PERSPECTIVES

A Multicultural Portrait of
Learning in America

By Petra Press

Marshall Cavendish
New York • London • Toronto

Cover: These kids enjoy learning in a school that integrates students of many backgrounds and abilities. Their class is far more open than classrooms in the early days of public schools.

Published by
Marshall Cavendish Corporation
2415 Jerusalem Avenue
P.O. Box 587
North Bellmore, New York 11710, USA

Edited, designed, and produced by Water Buffalo Books, Milwaukee

Project director: Mark Sachner
Art director: Sabine Beaupré
Picture researcher: Diane Laska
Editorial: Eileen Foran and Valerie Weber
Marshall Cavendish development editor: MaryLee Knowlton
Marshall Cavendish editorial director: Evelyn Fazio

Editorial consultant: Mark S. Guardalabene, Milwaukee Public Schools

Picture Credits: © Archive Photos: 11 (bottom), 13, 34, 39 (bottom); © Archive Photos/American Stock: 18; Sabine Beaupré: 70 (bottom); © The Bettmann Archive: 6, 9, 11 (top), 12, 15, 17, 20, 21, 24-25, 27, 28, 31 (both), 32, 33 (both), 36, 37, 38, 39 (top), 40, 41, 42, 44 (both), 45 (both), 46, 47, 48, 52, 53 (both), 54 (both), 55 (both), 56, 58 (top), 63, 65, 70 (top); © Culver Pictures, Inc.: 22; © Charles Phelps Cushing/H. Armstrong Roberts: 8; © S. Feld/H. Armstrong Roberts: 66; © Jeffry W. Myers/H. Armstrong Roberts: 62, 73; © David C. Phillips: 69, 74; © H. Armstrong Roberts: 51, 60-61; © Jim Wend: Cover, 58 (bottom), 68

Library of Congress Cataloging-in-Publication Data

Press, Petra.
    A multicultural portrait of learning in America / Petra Press.
        p.   cm. — (Perspectives)
    Includes bibliographical references (p.   ) and index.
    ISBN 1-85435-665-8 :
    1. Multicultural education—United States—History—Juvenile literature. [1. Multicultural education. 2. Minorities—Education. 3. Education—History.] I. Title. II. Series: Perspectives (Marshall Cavendish Corporation)
LC1099.3.P74   1994
370.19'6—dc20   93-48769
                                                                                                        CIP
                                                                                                        AC

To PS – MS

CONTENTS

About *Perspectives*

Perspectives is a series of multicultural portraits of events and topics in U.S. history. Each volume examines these events and topics not only from the perspective of the white European-Americans who make up the majority of the U.S. population, but also from that of the nation's many people of color and other ethnic minorities, such as African-Americans, Asian-Americans, Hispanic-Americans, and American Indians. These people, along with women, have been given little attention in traditional accounts of U.S. history. And yet their impact on historical events has been great.

The terms *American Indian, Hispanic-American, Latino, Anglo-American, Black, African-American,* and *Asian-American,* like *European-American* and *white,* are used by the authors in this series to identify people of various national origins. Labeling people is a serious business, and what we call a group depends on many things. For example, a few decades ago it was considered acceptable to use the words *colored* or *Negro* to label people of African origin. Today, these words are outdated and often a sign of ignorance or outright prejudice. Some even consider *Black* less acceptable than *African-American* because it focuses on a person's skin color rather than national origins. And yet *Black* has many practical uses, especially to describe people whose origins are not only African but Caribbean or Latin American as well.

If we must label people, it's better to be as specific as possible. That is a goal of *Perspectives* — to be as precise and fair as possible in the labeling of people by race, ethnicity, national origin, or other factors, such as gender, sexual orientation, or disability. When necessary and possible, Americans of Mexican origin will be called *Mexican-Americans*. Americans of Irish origin will be called *Irish-Americans*, and so on. The same goes for American Indians: when possible, specific Indians are identified by their tribal names, such as the *Chippewa* or *Mohawk*. But in a discussion of various Indian groups, tribal origins may not always be entirely clear, and so it may be more practical to use *American Indian*, a term that has widespread use among Indians and non-Indians alike.

Even within a group, individuals may disagree over the labels they prefer for their group: *Black* or *African-American? Hispanic* or *Latino? American Indian* or *Native American? White, Anglo,* or *European-American?* Different situations often call for different labels. The labels used in *Perspectives* represent an attempt to be fair, accurate, and perhaps most importantly, to be mindful of what people choose to call *themselves*.

A Note About *Learning in America*

For most of the last 350 years, educators in the United States have used the classroom as a mirror to reflect an image of a "white" America. Not only was that image a faulty and distorted reflection, it crippled the very resource that makes this nation strong: its cultural diversity. The Protestant, Anglo-American viewpoint of the events in U.S. history is and always has been just one perspective among many. Some estimate that by the year 2056, "minorities" will make up a majority or close to a majority of the U.S. population, and a strict Anglo-American perspective will in effect become the minority viewpoint. Yet until the last few decades, textbooks treated the contributions of non-European-Americans (and all women) as incidental and insignificant — if they included them at all. That's an amazing oversight when you consider that African-Americans have been an active part of this country's history since 1619, and that Asian-Americans have been here for over 150 years, long before most of the European immigrant groups arrived. Teachers would discuss U.S. westward expansion and barely touch on how it was shaped by Mexican-Americans, Blacks, Irish, Jews, or Chinese.

Not only were these minority cultures misrepresented in presentations of U.S. history, their children were denied equal educational opportunity. Colonists believed the only education women needed was learning how to keep house and read the Bible. Up until the 1860s, southern states enforced laws that made it illegal to contribute to the education of any Black person, slave or free. Spanish, French, and English missionaries kidnapped American Indians and forcibly taught them to read the Bible. There were no child labor laws in the mid-nineteenth century to prevent starving immigrant families from having to pull their children out of school in the sixth grade to work fourteen-hour days in city sweatshops. And as late as the mid-1950s, any school in the United States could (and did) legally keep minority students segregated from their European-American classmates.

Perhaps most distorted of all was the image education reflected of American Indian cultures. Only now are teachers beginning to present the real part they played in U.S. history and the devastating impact European cultures have had on theirs. Even more interesting is how these changes are creating an impact on the process of education itself. U.S. educators are now just discovering that "learning" is not memorization, discipline, and learning to conform. Rather, it is discovering how to survive by learning to understand our environment, how to appreciate and pass on the heritage of our diverse ancestry, and how to find our own path to spiritual awareness. It is understanding that human survival means working together as equal members of the same global community. Native American cultures have understood these simple concepts for thousands of years.

The struggle for equal educational opportunities for women, minorities, and people with disabilities was a long and often violent one that continues even today. This book is the story of that struggle.

Searching for his guardian spirit, a Navajo boy stops to rest on his vision quest,
a journey that will mark his transition to manhood.

CHAPTER ONE

Different Cultures Shape Early American Education

Oomaabe, a fourteen-year-old Winnebago boy, sits cross-legged on a grassy hilltop overlooking a moonlit river valley. Shivering in the predawn cold, he pulls the bearskin tighter around his shoulders and tries to ignore the knives of hunger stabbing his stomach. It's been four days since he's eaten, and he tries not to think of the roast duck and corn his mother cooked for him the night he left. His ankle throbs where he twisted it climbing through the fallen rocks, but when he hears the sudden, piercing howl of a not-so-distant wolf, he curses his broken bow more than his swollen ankle. For a moment, Oomaabe aches for the safety of his parents' warm teepee, but he quickly struggles to get these thoughts out of his mind and to concentrate instead on his quest. Looking up at the sliver of moon, he remembers the night of the summer solstice when the tribal elders had taken him aside and told him to prepare for this time. "You are old enough to form your own medicine now," they advised him. "It is time for you to search for your guardian spirit and to become a man." Fear and pride and excitement had coursed through his body like the icy rush of a mountain stream. Oomaabe knows this journey is a test of his worthiness. He knows he's ready to be shown his guardian spirit; after all, he's been preparing for this journey all of his life. He forgets his fears and resumes his prayer ritual to the Great Spirit.

American Indian Education Before the Arrival of the Europeans

In many Indian cultures, when a boy was considered old enough — and knowledgeable enough — by tribal elders, he would make this "vision" quest for a guardian spirit. (In some cultures, girls as well as boys went on this quest.) He would blacken his skin with charcoal and wander alone to a remote and secluded spot far from the tribe. For five or more days, he would go without food, brave the elements, and pray to the Great Spirit. During this period of danger and fasting, the first animal that he dreamed of when he fell asleep (or

The power of a name

Most Indian children were taught never to address anyone by his or her personal name. For many tribes, an Indian's real name was considered one's private, personal property. They believed that if an enemy knew and pronounced one's name out loud, he could gain control of one's soul. Most tribal members were therefore addressed by a title such as Brother, Uncle, or Warrior, or by a nickname. For example, Pocahontas, the famous Powhatan woman who saved the life of Captain John Smith, was really named Matowaka. (*Pocahontas* was a nickname that meant "frisky.")

It was not unusual for someone to have a number of different names over the course of a lifetime. If a member of the tribe committed a particularly brave or noble act, the tribe would give him a name to commemorate that honor. Often a youth who returned from a successful vision quest would be given a new name. A name could also hold supernatural powers. It was then passed down through generations as an inheritance and was regarded as both an honor and a responsibility that had to be lived up to.

that came to him in a waking vision) was the one the Great Spirit had chosen to be his special protector for life. If and when he achieved this vision, he returned to the tribal lodge and a great ceremony was held where he would tell everyone about his success.

The boy was now considered a man and given a new name. After eating a hearty meal, he would go out again, this time to hunt the animal about which he had dreamed. After killing the animal, he would skin it and then preserve and decorate the pelt, which he carried with him for the rest of his life as his guardian spirit. It was also buried with him when he died, to ensure his safe passage to the beautiful hunting grounds of the next world.

The spirit quest was an important rite of puberty — one of the ways American Indian cultures initiated their youth into adulthood — and it required years of study and preparation. Before the arrival of European missionaries, American Indians believed that the purpose of education was to teach their children to become responsible members of the tribal community. That meant that a young person had to meet strict requirements before he or she could be accepted as an adult. These requirements fell into three main categories: mastering specific survival skills, learning the tribe's cultural heritage, and achieving spiritual awareness.

Learning Survival Skills

Indian children began learning survival skills as soon as they could walk. These skills varied from tribe to tribe and from region to region and depended on whether the tribe was a hunting or a planting culture — or both. For example, although most of the Algonquin and Iroquois tribes of the Northeast Woodlands were agricultural, the cold weather and short growing season in the Northeast and around the Great Lakes also made them dependent on foraging for wild foods.

This meant that in addition to farming skills, Indian children were taught how to hunt fish and game and how to gather foods like maple syrup and wild rice. The men generally cleared the fields while the women did most of the actual farming. Girls were taught how to dress game, prepare food, tan hides, and sew clothing, while boys learned to hunt and fish. Boys were shown how to practice hunting with a bow as soon as they learned to walk and were often excellent marksmen by the time they were ten.

Many Indian boys not only practiced to become expert horsemen, they had to learn to capture and break wild ponies.

Native children also learned that survival depended not only on skills but on the proper attitude toward the earth and the beings living on it. All were taught the daily personal prayers and rituals that accompanied each of these tasks. They learned to have respect for the land and gratitude for the animals who gave up their lives to provide them with food.

Studying the Tribe's Language and Cultural Heritage

Another important part of childhood learning for American Indians was language and cultural heritage. Because cultures without a written language had to depend on an oral tradition, storytelling was the main way native children learned about their heritage. Certain members of the tribe's oldest generation were designated storytellers and were entrusted with the responsibility of transmitting this wealth of information to the youngest generation.

A different kind of discipline

Most American Indian cultures did not define "family" the same way traditional European cultures did. Children were not just raised and disciplined by their biological parents. In Indian societies, the extended family (grandparents, maternal uncles, paternal aunts, siblings, and cousins) and elder tribe members played an even greater role. Most tribes were *matrilineal,* which meant that the child always inherited the lineage of the mother. For example, a child of an Apache mother and Pueblo father would not be considered half Apache and half Pueblo, but rather, full Apache. It was always the mother and the mother's brothers (who lived nearby) who were responsible for disciplining the children. The father usually developed a close friendship with his children but had no say in their discipline. He was, however, obligated to discipline the children of his sisters.

European colonists for the most part did not hesitate to physically punish their children whenever they felt they needed it and were horrified by what Indians felt were more ingenious (and less abusive) methods. Indians rarely spanked or hit their children, because they believed that a child's ability to withstand pain without flinching was a sign of maturity. It was not logical to physically punish a child who was being taught by tribal ritual the nobility of enduring pain. Water was often used instead (ducking the child's head briefly in a bucket of water, or throwing water into the child's face). Mild ridicule by the child's peers was also an effective way of getting a mischievous older child to change his or her behavior. A naughty younger child might be scared into behaving with stories of supernatural beasties like child-eating screech owls.

Since storytelling required a keen memory, a sharp mind, and a respected presence, storytellers enjoyed prestigious positions within the community. They were also responsible for selecting and training those children who would grow up to be the tribe's next generation of storytellers.

Indian children learned more than just the exploits of their famous ancestors in these stories. Within the legends and fables were also more subtle lessons. They learned, for example, that those who developed courage, generosity, and kindness became leaders and that children who listened to old people, obeyed their parents, worked hard, and helped the poor grew up to be respected members of the community.

Although children were given plenty of opportunity to play and to explore their environment, their elders began their children's traditional tribal education as soon as they were able to talk. They quickly learned what types of behavior were considered taboo or forbidden. Everything they were taught was based on the underlying principles of honesty, courtesy, and respect: toward their elders, toward each other, and toward their natural environment. They were strictly advised not to stare at visitors (especially strangers) and never to address anyone by his or her personal name. One of the most rigorous parts of a child's education was learning to properly speak his or her native language. As soon as children learned to talk, every word they uttered was corrected until their grammar and pronunciation were perfect. Baby talk was not allowed. By the time a child was ten years old, he or she could speak as fluently as any adult.

The Importance of Spiritual Training

Another important part of childhood learning among American Indians stressed spiritual awareness. Whether they worshipped a creator or Great Spirit (such as *Taiowa* of the Hopi) or an all-powerful supernatural power (such as the *Wakan Tanka* of the Teton Sioux), almost all American Indians believed there was a creative force present in all living and nonliving things. They also believed that before a youth could be considered "mature," he or she must have completed a long apprenticeship of spiritual training.

The path to spiritual awareness was not an easy one. Children were shown at an early age by older mem-

The Mescalero Apache girls' puberty ceremony

Mescalero Apache girls in the Southwest still enter womanhood by participating in a special four-day puberty ritual that reenacts the Mescalero creation myths. The Circle of Life is used as a sort of blueprint for the ceremony. Each row of beads from the center outward symbolizes a song. Each girl has her own tribal singer, and the singers take turns singing the songs that tell the history of the tribe from its creation in the frozen north country in the time of nothingness up to the present. (Each year a new song is added.) The circle is also divided into four sections, simultaneously symbolizing the universe and its forces, the world and its four directions, nature and its four seasons, and the four stages of human life (infancy, childhood, adulthood, and old age). At the *kai*, or crosspoint, lies the fire pit at the center of the ceremonial. This point also represents the balance point of the universe. The girls and their singers dance, sing, and recreate the tribe's history for four days and four nights. On the fourth night, they stay up all night, after which the girls must run four times into the sunrise to the east to reenact the story of Changing Woman, who appeared in the east as a young girl and then disappeared in the west that same evening after aging to an infinite age — only to appear again the next morning in the east as a young women. With this last run, the girls affirm their capacity to create and to continue the tribe and so become women.

bers of the tribe how to participate in group rituals and ceremonies. The age of puberty was considered the dividing line between childhood and adulthood, and individual spiritual training became more intense as children neared the ages of twelve and thirteen. By this stage in life, an Indian boy was expected to be so courageous, skillful, and resourceful that he could live alone, if necessary, and be entirely self-sufficient.

In some cultures, making this transition involved a vision quest in search of a guardian spirit; in others, the child was required to go through a long and often physically painful initiation ceremony. Preparation for either the initiation ceremony or the vision quest required years of training that included long stretches of fasting and prayer, cold morning baths in icy streams, mastering complicated ceremonial rites, and learning to endure intense physical pain.

While each tribal culture had its own religious ceremonies and social customs, all shared the belief that their children were the lifeblood of the community and that the survival of tribal culture and traditions depended on the strength of future generations. They also believed that the proper education of the tribe's children was the responsibility and primary concern of every member of the tribe, not just the children's parents. By the time Indian children reached adulthood (at about fourteen), their survival skills, their interest in preserving their tribe's culture and traditions, and their spiritual awareness gave them the tools they needed to face any kind of hardship. Few of the Europeans who came to colonize North America were aware of the depth or intensity of the education American Indians provided their children.

The Arrival of European Colonists

When the first European explorers set foot in North America in the fifteenth century, they brought back stories of a paradise rich in furs and gold. In the following centuries, Spain, Portugal, Holland, England, France, Germany, and even Russia were all anxious to expand their empires and claim as much of this "New World" as they could for themselves. European colonists came for a number of reasons. Some came to make their fortunes. Some belonged

Ceremonies like the *you-pel-lay,* or green corn dance (top), were a sacred responsibility carefully passed on from a tribe's elders to its younger generation. Many historical portrayals of Native American culture came from artists traveling with the U.S. Army (bottom). The accuracy of these portraits depended on the attitudes of the European-American artists who created them.

To the Pilgrims, spirituality meant worshipping in church and studying the Bible.

to groups trying to escape religious or political persecution. Some came as indentured servants hoping to buy back their freedom or as criminals whose sentences were shortened if they agreed to serve them in the colonies. And some also came as missionaries to convert the Indians to Christianity.

Although Indian cultures had their own highly developed ideas of spiritual and practical education, it was based on a value system Europeans did not understand. In most cases, European settlers insisted on trying to convert Indians to their own religious and social values and force them to speak their language. This was not only true in the original thirteen colonies along the Atlantic coast, but in the Spanish, French, and even Russian colonies to the south and west as well.

Spanish Colonies of the Southwest

Spain was the first European power to gain a stronghold in the North American West by conquering and enslaving the local Pueblo, Yanqui, and Yuma Indians. Eventually, Spanish colonists realized that their colonial outposts north of the Rio Grande were too isolated from supplies and protection from the Spanish stronghold in Mexico City and that they were going to need help from the local Indians if they wanted to survive. The Catholic Church, the cornerstone of life and education for Spanish colonists, was also becoming concerned about Spain's brutal treatment of the Indians. So, in the 1760s, the Spanish began setting up missions in the Southwest and along the California coast to convert the Indians to Catholicism. These missions controlled land, livestock, and labor and radically changed the way thousands of Indians of this region lived. The Franciscan missionaries intended to do more than convert them to Christianity, however. They meant to make the Indians live what they considered to be more orderly and disciplined lives.

They did teach the Indians a wide variety of new skills, such as weaving, blacksmithing, and bricklaying. The Indians living on missions learned how to raise sheep, cattle, horses, and goats. Many were taught to read in an effort to convert them to Catholicism. But the effect on Indian life was horrifying. The Indians did not perform this work voluntarily for the Spanish missionaries. It was forced labor. If they resisted or tried to escape, they were publicly whipped by Spanish soldiers or thrown into irons. This harsh discipline, combined with a poor diet, inadequate sanitation, and lack of medical care, made Indians on missions particularly susceptible to disease. During the period when Spanish missions flourished in California, the Indian population between San Diego and San Francisco declined from seventy-two thousand to eighteen thousand.

Among the Spanish themselves, there was, ironically, less of an effort made to teach or train colonists, and only the wealthy could afford to educate their children by hiring tutors or sending them to school in Spain.

Education in the French Colonies

The French did most of their exploring in North America along river routes and therefore interacted most often with Indian nations and cultures that could be reached via these waterways. The first French explorer in North America was Jacques Cartier, who sailed up the St. Lawrence River in 1534. By 1682, another French explorer, Sieur de La Salle (Robert Cavelier), had traveled by birch canoe all the way down the Mississippi River from the Great Lakes to the Gulf of Mexico, claiming all the land in between for France. France, however, was far more interested in dominating the fur trade than in establishing colonies in this territory. Few of the French explorers or trappers brought their wives and families with them to set up communities in the "New World."

The French interacted with many of the Algonquin and Iroquois tribes of the Great Lakes area, as well as the Blackfoot, Cheyenne, Crow, Sioux, and Wichita of the Great Plains. Catholic missionaries often went along with French traders on their explorations of new river routes. While they also came to North America to convert the Indians to Christianity, the Jesuit priests tended to treat Indians more humanely than the Spanish missionaries did. They also had a greater respect for Indian culture.

While the Spanish would accept white-Indian marriages if they had to, they basically considered American Indians to be pagan and inferior. Most of the French explorers and traders, on the other hand, had respect for Indian life and an interest in Indian language and culture. They often adopted Indian customs and intermarried with local tribes (although a number of French traders exploited Indians by taking Indian women back to France as slaves).

Before trying to convert local Indians to Christianity and teaching them French language and customs, Jesuit missionaries did their best to learn native languages, customs, and beliefs. Unlike the Franciscans who set up the Spanish missions in the Southwest, the Jesuits did not force whole families to live on missions. Instead, they removed Indian children from their families and tribes and brought them to the missions to live while they were being educated. The education they received, however, was the same

Explorer Sieur de La Salle claims the Mississippi Valley for France. The French interacted with Indians along the many waterways they explored as France sought to build a fur-trading empire in North America.

education the French colonists offered their own children. In addition to religion, learning to read and write French, and French customs, Indian children studied a variety of other academic subjects, such as agriculture, singing, and carpentry.

Although most Indians had no interest in Christianity, they put up with the Jesuits at first for several important reasons. They were curious about European technology and medicine, and they saw the French as potential allies against warring tribes. Furthermore, anyone who was not an enemy was considered a guest and had to be treated as such. They believed it would have been rude not to listen.

The Pacific Northwest

The fur trade is also what brought the French, British, and Russians to the rich forests and farmlands of the Pacific Northwest. French Jesuits tried to convert local tribes (including the Cayus and Nez Perce Indians) to Catholicism, the Russians set up Russian Orthodox missions, the British sent Anglican missionaries, and, later, even the U.S. sent Methodists, Presbyterians, Congregationalists, and Episcopalians. For the Indians, the conflict and hostility between all of these Protestant and Catholic sects made them leery about Christianity in general.

A few of these missionaries did at least have the best interests of the Indians at heart, with plans to build schools to teach the Indians advanced agriculture and animal husbandry. Unfortunately, there was so much bickering and feuding between the different factions that few of the schools were ever built.

The quality of life the Indians were forced to endure in these missions was so terrible that many were killed trying to escape, while others killed their own newborn children rather than have them grow up under such cruel tyranny. Not only were the Indians forced to give up their own cultures and religion in favor of Christianity, they were forced to work the fields to support the missions. As on the Spanish missions of the Southwest, refusal to work meant deprivation of food; being absent from church or religious classes meant corporal punishment and solitary confinement.

For most of the children of the trappers and traders in the Pacific Northwest, education meant learning at home or, at best, a one-room, frontier schoolhouse in which a single school master or school marm taught grades one through eight at the same time. Lessons were based on reading the Bible, and children were basically just taught the three "Rs": reading, writing, and arithmetic. Teachers were also given the authority to administer physical discipline to the students.

Indian Education, European-style, in the Original Thirteen Colonies

The first permanent British settlements in North America began at Plymouth Colony in 1620 with a tiny community of Separatist Puritans who chose to call themselves Pilgrims. A neighboring colony, Massachusetts Bay, was also

Most one-room colonial school houses were not pleasant or comfortable places for children to learn.

made up of Puritans, although this sect did not officially separate from the Church of England.

In spite of their cultural differences, Indians believed at first that they could live peacefully with the Puritans. Problems arose when these colonists tried to impose their Christian lifestyles on cultures that held a totally different value system. The native Algonquin tribes, for example, already had a well-ordered society with an impressive and complex system of government and a highly developed culture of arts and crafts. They were satisfied with their culture and didn't see any good reason for becoming more like the British. The Algonquins, like other Native Americans, showed a reverence for all aspects of nature and believed that their spiritual leaders receive guidance from unseen spirits — and that these spirits are everywhere: in caves, in springs, in trees, and in animals. (In fact, many Indians believed that there had once been a golden age when humans and animals lived and talked together.) Many of the first Puritans regarded these beliefs as sacrilegious. They believed that the Iroquois and Algonquin they encountered were harmless and childlike primitives who could (and should) be remolded to fit the Christian European version

Indian contributions to the English language

When European explorers and colonists arrived in North America, there were hundreds of plants and animals and even weather phenomena they had never seen before. From the beginning, Europeans borrowed words American Indians used. *Moose, caribou, raccoon, opossum, chipmunk, barracuda, manatee, cougar, puma, jaguar, terrapin, chigger,* and *skunk* are all Indian words for animals that have found their way into the English language. Indian words we now use for trees and plants include *hickory, pecan, persimmon, mahogany, mangrove, mesquite, yucca,* and *saguaro.* Foods include *maize* (corn), *hominy, squash, avocado, pemmican, cassava, papaya, pawpaw, tapioca, succotash,* and *scuppernong.* American Indian words that entered the English language via Spanish include *cigar, tobacco, tomato,* and *hammock.* Some language experts even believe the American expression *okay* was derived from the Choctaw word *oke,* meaning "it is so."

of civilization. Efforts to educate them started almost immediately, but there was some disagreement about the way to go about it.

From 1607 to 1622, the Virginia Council worked on a plan that called for kidnapping as many Algonquin children as possible and shipping them to England, to be educated in English homes. Policymakers in England, on the other hand, wanted the colonists to educate Indian children themselves. Although the English policymakers won out, little was actually done in the seventeenth century colonial period to do more than convert Indians to Christianity. The colonists were too busy just trying to survive in those first years to have time to take in reluctant Indian children.

Converting Indians to Christianity, however, did mean first teaching them to read. In 1649, an organization called "The Society for the Propagation of the Gospel in New England" was created to do just that. The society established Indian schools in what they called the "praying towns," guarded settlements where colonists relocated converted Indians to protect them from so-called hostile Indians who were still resisting conversion and to prevent them from lapsing into their previous, supposedly sinful lifestyle. In other New England communities, Indian children attended the regular town grammar schools with colonial children.

Because the Puritans quickly got carried away in their zeal to remake the Indians, these early, peaceful missionary attempts did not last long. By the early 1800s, Indians had come to resent the Europeans' self-righteous and patronizing attitudes and eventually responded with open hostility. The colonists' missionary enthusiasm deteriorated into contempt and suspicion. By the end of the eighteenth century, the only religious sects that continued to promote the missionary education of Indians were the Morovians, the Episcopalians, and a few Calvinists.

The Middle Atlantic colonies (Delaware, New Jersey, New York, and Pennsylvania) had an even greater diversity of religions and nationalities than New England had. Settlers from Holland, Germany, Sweden, England, Wales, and Scotland all came to the Middle Atlantic colonies in large numbers, and the area became a haven for people escaping from religious persecution.

Mennonites, Quakers, Lutherans, Calvinists, Catholics, Jews, Morovians, Huguenots, Separate Baptists, and Episcopalians were just a few of the many religious groups that set up schools in the colonies. This area also had the most rapid growth of urban areas and a healthy interaction of commerce and trade. All of these factors combined to make the schools in these colonies much more open to intellectual freedom and growth than other North American colonies.

Their attitudes toward the education of Indians and African-Americans were also more liberal. The Quakers, for example, believed not only in the equality of women but in the equality of people of all races, and opened many of their school doors to Indians. The Friends, as Quakers were called, actively included Indians in their schools, made books available to Indian communities, and established minority apprenticeship programs. Other denominations also became active in providing educational opportunities for Indians, such as the Morovians and the Methodists.

Attitudes in the Thirteen Colonies Toward the Education of African-Americans

As with Native Americans, early colonial concern for educating African slaves arose mainly from Christian missionaries. African-Americans played an important part in the development of the thirteen colonies right from the beginning. The great movement of Africans to North America began in the early 1500s, when boatloads of Africans were brought as slaves into the West Indies, primarily by the Dutch.

Shortly after that, Africans were brought into Spanish colonies in Mexico and South and Central America. In 1619, the first Africans were brought into the British colonies, giving their descendants an older American heritage than that claimed by descendants of the Pilgrims who came over on the *Mayflower*.

The Dutch captain who brought the first African immigrants sold them as indentured servants, but they were quickly reduced to slave status. For the next two hundred years, more and more Africans were brought into the Americas to labor in the fields to produce such crops as tobacco, cotton, rice, and sugar. Not all African-Americans in the early colonies were slaves, however. In 1790, shortly after the thirteen colonies became the United States, there were sixty thousand free Blacks in the country. Nor were all slaves or indentured servants necessarily Black. Indians were often taken as slaves by the colonists, and many British convicts were shipped to the colonies on the Atlantic coast to serve out their sentences as indentured servants.

An early American slave market. Early colonists did not believe their African-American slaves needed an education.

From their owners' points of view, African-Americans slaves in New England did not need any other type of education (although later, when the owners of slaves believed it would be profitable for their own businesses, they had their slaves learn various agricultural, mechanical, household, and business skills). But the same attitudes did not necessarily apply toward free Blacks. In most northern communities, Blacks had access either to public schools or to private schools operated by special charity organizations and abolitionist (anti-slavery) societies.

By contrast, education was much less available to free Blacks in the Southeast. Another factor in the North that contributed to African-American opportunities for education was the apprentice system. Before 1830, it was required by law that all apprentices, regardless of the trade, be first taught to read and write.

The Southern colonies had rigid social class distinctions that allowed few educational opportunities for indentured servants, slaves, or poor freemen. There were no schools to provide the skills needed to operate farms and plantations. The exceptions were apprenticeship education and the efforts of charity organizations on behalf of the poor, the Indians, and the slaves, so the little education that was made available was provided strictly at the whim of the wealthy and powerful. Also, unlike the North, the South did not have laws requiring that apprentices first be taught to read and write.

General Attitudes Toward Education in the Thirteen Colonies

Although the European colonies that later united to form the United States were supposedly based on principles of equality and democracy, the educational opportunities they offered were far from being either equal or democratic. Social status, race, sex, religion, and even geographic area were all factors that determined how much a child was allowed to learn.

The children of the wealthy, especially on the rich plantations of the South, received the best educational opportunities. Slaves, indentured servants, and the very poor (whether they were of American Indian, African, Asian, or even European descent) were often denied even the chance to learn to read and write.

In most of the colonies, young girls, it was felt, did not need a formal education; they only needed to learn the Bible and the skills needed to manage a household and family. And children with physical,

Teaching a classroom of ten-year-olds, even in a mission school like the one shown here, sometimes felt like a hopeless task.

psychological or emotional disabilities were rarely given any educational consideration at all.

Strong Emphasis on Religion and Social Class. Most colonists agreed that schools should be based on religious principles, but since they could never have agreed on whose religious principles, the various religious denominations controlled their own schools. Also, the governments of the colonies in the 1700s did not have the tax money to run public schools. Therefore, private individuals and religious organizations were usually allowed to set up schools of their own without government interference.

Like their European counterparts, colonial schools before the 1770s were class-oriented and not very democratic. Although it was much easier for ambitious men in the colonies to rise up to a higher social and economic class than it was in Europe at the time, it was not equal educational opportunity that opened those doors, but hard work in a time when there was much work to be done. Most lower-class settlers had very little chance to get more than a basic education.

Early colonists had to struggle just to produce food and build some sort of community. They were less interested in having their children learn Latin grammar than master the basics of hunting, farming, or a skilled trade. A common practice among working-class (and some middle-class) parents was to apprentice their sons to skilled tradesmen or shopkeepers for several years to learn the skills of a trade. Even in the South, where wealthy plantation owners often hired tutors or sent their children to English schools, most early colonists planned their schools mainly to teach the basics of reading, writing, and religion.

The Importance of Discipline. Most of the Protestant religious sects that settled in the thirteen colonies (particularly the Puritans) believed that children were born evil and that only the strictest of disciplined upbringings could put them on the path to salvation. They believed that children should learn to fear God and shun the devil and that they should be taught the value of hard work, a frugal lifestyle, and the importance of acquiring material possessions. Children should also be taught respect for authority and the rights and property of others, as well as neatness, punctuality, honesty, and patriotism.

The best way to do this, they felt, was for everyone to study the Bible. At first, the Pilgrims insisted parents educate their children in their own homes. But by 1642, Massachusetts decided that most parents were neglecting that responsibility and passed a law requiring education for all. In 1647, Massachusetts took stronger measures, requiring every town to either set up a school or pay its share of costs to run a school in the nearest larger town.

The curriculum of the typical town school consisted of the four "Rs": reading, writing, arithmetic — and religion. Both boys and girls entered school at the age of six or seven, beginning their lessons with an early reader called a hornbook and then moving on to study the *New England Primer*, a crudely illustrated reader that contained grotesque pictures of religious saints being burned at the stake. Many children only remained in school for three

Many types of schools in the thirteen colonies

Left: Oil painting *The Country School*, 1871, by Winslow Homer.

Town schools. Very few girls were allowed to enroll in town schools. Those who did had to wait with their lessons until the boys received theirs first. In some towns, the custom was to have the girls attend at hours when the boys were not present, such as early in the morning or during the boys' summer vacations. The curriculum was usually the four "Rs": religion, reading, writing, and arithmetic.

Dame schools. While the dame school was open to girls, its most important function was to give little boys the basic English they would need to attend the town schools. Many of these schools were entirely private, getting the name "dame school" because they were held in the home of a school dame or mistress. The curriculum was simple. While all students learned the alphabet, some spelling and reading, and arithmetic, girls were also taught sewing and knitting.

Adventure schools (for girls). In the eighteenth century, many of the larger colonial cities started offering girls an alternative to the town schools. So-called adventure masters offered instruction in social accomplishments such as music and dancing, fancy needlework, fencing, violin lessons, French, and painting. Because some of these schools also taught reading, writing, and basic arithmetic, adventure schools often gave girls a better education than they could get at the town schools.

Dutch schools. What is now New York State was originally a Dutch colony called New Netherlands. In the early days of the colony, the Dutch West Indies Company took it upon itself to provide schools in the nine chartered villages of New Netherlands. (the biggest one being New Amsterdam, a city later renamed New York). Later, when English became the dominant influence, the same Dutch schools continued to exist, but became private parochial schools supported by local churches.

Quaker schools. Quaker schools in Pennsylvania became known for their quality education. They taught reading, writing, arithmetic, and bookkeeping as well as religion, and they were never closed to either girls or the poor. Quaker teachers were the first in the U.S. to receive teacher training. Baptists, Morovians, and Presbyterians set up similar schools.

Academies. The academy was a secondary school established in the Middle Atlantic colonies to prepare students for a trade. Academies offered courses in such subjects as trade, merchandising, navigation, and mechanics. Benjamin Franklin opened one of the first academies in Pennsylvania in 1751, a school that became a model for many others.

The Latin grammar schools. These were secondary schools set up in the Middle Atlantic colonies to prepare students (men only) who could afford to go on to college. Teachers in these schools were mostly ministers who had no church to serve, and they taught Greek and Latin as well as classical literature. Although many different religions offered Latin schools (and there was freedom of choice), schools were often used to promote religious propaganda that criticized other religions, especially Catholicism.

The common school. For the most part, private secondary education was only open to the wealthier classes who could afford it. There were exceptions, however. In Philadelphia, for example, a night school was founded in 1731 that offered classes in navigation, surveying, and mathematics to the sons of middle-class workingmen and artisans.

Because colonists were becoming increasingly hungry for knowledge, public lectures were given on natural science, astronomy, and mechanics, and private circulating libraries were established that allowed the public to borrow books for a fee.

Left: Most of what passed for learning for early European-Americans was boring and repetitious — either reading monotonous texts out loud or worse, memorizing them.

Old field schools. Old field schools were run in the South by local communities to teach poor children the basics of reading and writing. They were generally built on a worn-out field that was part of a local plantation and were conducted for just a few months out of every year.

Charity schools. In the southern United States, the Anglican Church raised funds in England to buy books and establish schools for the sole purpose of teaching orphans and paupers. These schools were called charity schools.

Jewish schools. Religious instruction has always been important to Jewish education. But early Jewish communities placed setting up cemeteries, places of worship, and aid to the poor above religious teaching, and it was not until 1808 that the first Jewish school came into being. This school met afternoons and Sundays to supplement academies and Latin grammar schools. Jewish kids were thus able to take advantage of the social benefits that education gave them and learn enough Jewish tradition to be sure their culture survived.

Below: Many Puritans believed women's brains were not strong enough to handle more than reading the Bible and learning efficient household skills.

or four years. Those who stayed longer went on to read the Book of Psalms, the Bible, and whatever other suitable books were available. Books and paper were scarce and students usually had to write out their lessons on slate tablets and then memorize them. They were not encouraged to ask questions or to express opinions. Schools generally operated six days a week, except during the summer.

Educational Opportunities for Women

Most of the early colonists believed that women could find all the wisdom they would ever need in a daily study of their scriptures and that they certainly did not need or deserve the opportunity for educational advancement. (The Puritans actually believed that women's brains were not strong enough for learning and that they became easily "unbalanced" pursuing abstract ideas.)

There were, of course, many women in this early colonial period who pursued a higher education anyway — in secret and on their own. One such woman, Mrs. John Quincy Adams, was an avid reader of French and English literature as well as ancient and modern

The changing role of women

In the Middle Atlantic colonies, being a wife and mother was not always a woman's sole function. Many women, mostly for economic reasons, practiced a trade or started their own businesses. Typical occupations included storekeeping, teaching, sewing, spinning, making gloves, acting as midwives, and manufacturing all sorts of items from "ointment for the itch" to powder and wigs. They took up nursing, professional cake baking, running laundries, delicatessens, and hat shops, brewing beer, and even publishing newspapers.

philosophy. (As an adult, however, she was always careful to point out that she would have understood the material better if she had been born with a male brain.)

There were few educational opportunities open to girls in the original thirteen colonies. In New England, some girls were allowed to enroll in town schools and dame schools (so named because they were held in the home of a school dame, or mistress). Larger cities went a small step further and developed "adventure schools" to offer girls a more social education by the end of the eighteenth century. Although religious attitudes toward women were more liberal in the Middle Atlantic colonies, they did not greatly increase women's educational opportunities. The Quakers, for example, not only believed that all *men* were created equal, but that the same divine inner light that existed in males also existed in females. The purpose of education was to make each member of the Quaker faith a minister of God's word, and both men and women were entitled to that education. Quakers established elementary schools, promoted apprenticeship training in some craft or trade, and demanded a strict religious training and moral upbringing for children of both sexes.

The Quakers were not the only religious sect to hold such views. The Morovians believed that women were every bit as capable as men and set up their schools accordingly. But even in Quaker society, the chief goal of a young woman was to get married, and the everyday tasks they learned to run a household were similar to those practiced by European-American women in New England.

Education During the Revolution – Not a Priority

As the colonies became more prosperous and independent, the focus of education was beginning to shift from religion to farming and trading, while the focus of the colonists was shifting from local community issues to more pressing national problems. During the years the colonists fought for their independence, most schools were closed completely. Not until the early nineteenth century did the U.S. as a nation turn its attention to the problem of providing good schools.

Pratt's Training and Industrial School for Indian children in Carlisle, Pennsylvania. "I believe in immersing Indians in our civilization," said founder Colonel Richard Pratt, "and when we get them under, holding them there until they are thoroughly soaked."

CHAPTER TWO

Learning in a Growing Nation

Lone Wolf, a shy Blackfoot boy growing up on a Montana Indian reservation in the 1880s, did not have happy memories of going to school. When he was eight, he was taken by force to an Indian boarding school hundreds of miles away. The government agents just showed up one bitter cold day, rounded up as many of the Blackfoot children as they could, loaded them onto wagons, and drove them across the state to Fort Shaw. Lone Wolf remembered how all of the children cried. Like him, they had never been separated from their parents or community before, and they were scared and confused. The parents, who were powerless to stop the soldiers, stood paralyzed with grief, unable even to wave as the wagons drove off with their children.

For Lone Wolf, the situation became even more horrifying after the long journey was over and they finally reached the bleak, isolated school. After separating the boys and girls into different buildings, the first thing their new instructors did was strip the children of all their clothes and belongings (anything that could remind them of their Blackfoot identity and of home), pile them up in a heap outside, and set them on fire. They even took away the little medicine bag Lone Wolf's mother had given him to protect him from harm. The next humiliation was getting his hair cut off — the thick black braids that were already growing as long and beautiful as those of the tribe's most noble warriors. They changed how he looked that first day; they even changed how he spoke. It was forbidden to speak anything but English at the school, and the new boys soon learned that anyone caught talking in his native tongue would be strapped with a leather belt until he could hardly walk.

Lone Wolf found the daily regimentation and cruel discipline of the school unbearable, but the lonely nights without his family were worse. At first, all he could think about was running away, but he soon realized that those who tried were almost always caught and brought back by the local police. One February evening, when they were standing in line for supper, one of the boys whispered something in his native language to the boy ahead of him. The man in charge of watching them immediately grabbed him and threw him across the room with such force that he broke the boy's collarbone. No one knew how he could possibly have heard about the incident, but the next day the boy's father showed up. Shaking with anger, the old Indian warrior told the school's instructors that Blackfoot children were never to be punished by striking them but were disciplined instead with kind words and good examples. Before the astounded instructors could stop him, the old warrior grabbed his son and disappeared from the school grounds.

Lone Wolf knew that they would have to run far away from the soldiers to escape, maybe even to Canada. But even so, as he lay awake that night on his cot in the cold, dark dorm room with thirty other boys, he envied them. They were free.

Changing Attitudes Toward Indian Education in the Nineteenth Century

The treatment American Indians received at the hands of European colonists grew worse when the U.S. gained its independence and started spreading westward. The efforts the early colonists made in the 1600s and 1700s to educate Indians had failed because they didn't realize how complex and sophisticated Indian cultures were. They had no idea of the depth of the spiritual, cultural, and practical education Indian families gave their children, or how important tribal instruction was to every aspect of their lives. It's not that Indian philosophy was too complicated for European colonists to understand. On the contrary, it was basically very simple.

To most American Indians, education was not just learning certain skills or acquiring specific knowledge, it was literally learning how to be a human being and how to develop one's character to its highest spiritual degree. They knew that without this spiritual core, people would use knowledge and skills for personal gain, even if it meant hurting other people. But the colonists believed they had failed because they didn't transform the Indians into copies of themselves: Christian capitalists with perfect (that is, European) manners. The approach these colonists used to interact with Indian cultures had even more disastrous effects in the years following American independence.

Education Within the Five Civilized Tribes

After the U.S. gained its independence, the five most powerful tribes in the Southeast — the Cherokee, Choctaw, Chickasaw, Creek, and Seminole — felt that to continue to survive in the changing "New World," they would need to assimilate into European-American culture. Often called the Five

Civilized Tribes of the Southeast, they used the ruling European-American government and culture as a model and drafted laws, elected constitutional governments, set up missionary schools for their children, and practiced the most modern farming methods. Many went so far in copying white culture that they bought and kept African-American slaves.

In spite of these Indian efforts at "civilization," southern states began demanding that the federal government remove the Five Tribes further west to territories in

The Seminoles, one of the most powerfu! tribes in the Southeast before being removed to Indian Territory in the 1830s, drafted laws, elected governments, and set up schools for their children.

Nebraska, Kansas, and Oklahoma. The southern states not only wanted tribal lands for themselves, they did not want Indians (or Blacks or any other minority) assimilated into their culture. Any chances the Five Tribes had of escaping the fate of removal were lost when Andrew Jackson was inaugurated as president in 1829. It was well known that he opposed Indian rights, and after he was elected, he publicly refused to honor federal treaty obligations that protected these southern tribes from removal. In the spring of 1830, he pushed his Indian Removal Act through Congress, and the Five Tribes were told they would be "removed" to federal Indian Territory in Oklahoma.

The Choctaw: Pioneers of bilingual education

Many minority groups today are arguing for bilingual and bicultural education, but few realize these are not new ideas. The Choctaw had a successful bilingual and bicultural educational system over 130 years ago when they still lived on their lands in Mississippi. Their system moved with them even after they were removed to Indian Territory (in present-day Oklahoma) in 1830. By the early 1800s, their leaders realized they had only three options left to them: wage war on the U.S. government, assimilate into white society, or face removal. They choose assimilation. Because so many French and English colonists had intermarried into the Choctaw Nation over the years, their influence helped convince the government that Choctaw schools would be much more successful! if they could teach children first in their native language and then slowly convert to English. They would also start with Indian culture and then slowly introduce the so-called advantages of European-American culture. These schools were closed during the Civil War war so the schools could be used

to house Confederate soldiers, but they reopened again once the war was over.

The Choctaws' bilingual and bicultural education had a big impact. Because of their knowledge of U.S. culture and government, the Choctaw were able to survive under their own rule until 1897, longer than nearly all other Indian nations. During the late 1800s, the Choctaw stayed loyalty to their way of life. At the same time they produced attorneys, physicians, ministers, and businessmen who in turn brought the benefits of their Anglo-American education back to benefit the Choctaw people. The Choctaw printed bilingual newspapers that covered national issues and even maintained a staff in Washington, D.C., to represent their tribal interests. The only mistake the Choctaw made was in trusting the U.S. government to be as fair and honest in their dealings as the Choctaw were. They were horrified to learn in 1893 that the newly formed Dawes Commission was about to dissolve the Choctaw Nation and confiscate its land.

The Choctaw were the first of the Five Civilized Tribes to make the long journey in 1831. They were forced to march from Mississippi to Oklahoma barefoot, starving, and under guard, through blizzards and subzero temperatures. The Creek were next, leaving Alabama in 1836. Nearly half of the Creek nation died on the march or during their first year in exile. In 1837, the Cherokee began a removal that would take them two years to complete. The losses they suffered through sickness and exposure to the severe weather were staggering. Over thirty thousand Indians died making the journey or shortly after reaching Oklahoma.

The Choctaw and Cherokee continued their efforts to develop formal Indian education even after their removal from their homelands in the Southeast. They designed their own school system and developed a network of over two hundred classrooms in Oklahoma in the 1830s. Tribal literacy rose by 90 percent. A long tradition of Cherokee journalism began with the founding of the *Cherokee Phoenix,* which was published in both native and English languages. Tribal elders explained to younger members of the community that education was important because they would be constantly dealing with white people, and unless they learned to speak their language and to read and write as they do, white people would always be able to cheat them.

Originally, U.S. treaties guaranteed that the area now encompassing Oklahoma, Kansas, and Nebraska would remain a permanent Indian territory. But by the 1840s, when the U.S. had acquired Texas, California, and Oregon and non-Indian settlers were heading west by the thousands and grabbing up all of the available land, it became apparent that a permanent Indian territory was not going to work.

The Carlisle Indian School band. Involvement in school band and sports activities did not make the loneliness or harsh military discipline of Indian boarding schools any easier to endure.

Government Boarding Schools Created for Indian Children

At about the same time, an increasing number of Christian whites were trying to "reform" Indians through education. They believed that if they took Indian children and taught them white habits of hygiene, diet, and clothing, taught them to work by the clock and worship God on Sundays, the problems of Indian poverty and dependency would eventually disappear. In 1819, Congress set aside what it called a Civilization Fund to allow church groups to teach Indian children "habits of morality and industry." This led to the creation of a system of government-subsidized boarding schools for Indian children. By 1838, there were about eighty of these schools in the U.S.

Military-like dress and discipline were the norm in these boarding schools. At first, they were located close enough to the students' villages to allow for occasional visits. But after a while, the stricter educators decided that Indian

Neither Indian nor white

Many of the Indian students who attended government boarding schools often found that after they graduated they had nowhere to go. Some tried to return to their communities, but fellow tribe members often treated them as though they were foreigners, even after putting them through harsh reentry ordeals. Although they had learned valuable occupational skills as students (such as printing, blacksmithing, and farming), most were not happy living and working in a white culture that treated them as less than second-class citizens. Sun Elk, an Arizona Pueblo, later wrote about coming home to his father's house after spending seven long years in the Carlisle Indian School he was forced to attend in Pennsylvania. His parents were stunned and saddened to see the strange youth that used to be their beautiful son. Dressed in white man's clothes with short, carefully combed hair, Sun Elk could remember only a few words of his native Pueblo. He even smelled strange. Faced with the sad rejection of his family and the hostile stares of other tribe members, Sun Elk walked away from his family's village and spent the next several years finding work in white man's towns in Wyoming and Colorado, sick in heart and spirit. But Sun Elk was one of the luckier boarding school graduates. When his tribe was forced to divide up its lands after 1900, he took the money he had saved and bought some of the farm land. But it wasn't until he eventually married an orphan Pueblo that he was accepted back into the tribe. Then he let his hair grow and put on the tribal blankets — glad to be an Indian again.

children needed to be completely separated from their roots and preferred to transport them halfway across the continent to a boarding school, if that was at all possible. A Sioux writer named Luther Standing Bear wrote of his memories of Indian children traveling by train to a boarding school in the East. These kids were so homesick and so scared that they started singing the death songs Sioux warriors traditionally sang only when going into battle.

The boarding school experience was traumatizing for parents, too. In traditional Indian culture, the tribal unit was even more important than the nuclear family. When the younger members of the tribe were missing from crucial religious festivals or the initiation rituals that transformed them into adults, the parents knew that the continuation of the culture itself was in jeopardy. They also knew that one of the main aims of the boarding school was to convince children to turn their backs on their traditional cultures. Indian parents had other important concerns about boarding schools. They were outraged by the forced recruitment and cruel treatment of the children, but their outrage did little to stop the mistreatment.

Indian Education After the Civil War

After the Civil War, during the presidency of Ulysses S. Grant, the federal government tried to turn over its responsibility for Indian welfare to religious organizations such as the Protestants, Catholics, and Quakers. By 1872, for example, Presbyterians took over nine agencies that had jurisdiction over thirty-eight thousand Indians, and Catholics had seven agencies overseeing eighteen thousand Indians. This shift of responsibility was part of Grant's so-called Peace Policy and was designed to eliminate the corruption and terrible abuses in the government administration of Indian reservations. In actuality, it had the opposite effect.

Although for years government money had been allocated for food, clothing, farming tools, and other necessary reservation supplies, very few of these goods ever actually made it to people living on the reservations, who were by this time living in poverty. Not only were Indians not even consulted on this new change in policy, but there was no noticeable change under the new policy in how supplies were distributed. The celebrated Peace Policy did not even produce peace. Some of the bloodiest battles between Indians and the U.S. government (such as the battle at Little Big Horn) took place in the 1870s after the policy was enacted. But the drive to forcibly educate Indian children continued, Peace Policy or not, and so did the practice of sending them to boarding schools. It was not until about 1900 that Indian children would begin to enroll in regular public schools.

The Great Educational Awakening

The schooling of Indian children was not the only educational issue that caused controversy in the nineteenth century. During the late 1700s, when the colonists were fighting for their independence from Britain, people had very little time to worry about education. Most schools were closed because of a shortage of teachers, books, and money, and the more urgent matter of the war against Britain. When the charity schools closed their doors, there was no general outcry of concern. For the most part, educational opportunities had only been available to the wealthy, and there was more of a protest when the better private schools began to close down. But this, too, was overshadowed by the more urgent concerns of the Revolutionary War. (The Constitution, which was so carefully written in 1776, does not even mention education, let alone guarantee or provide for it.) In fact, education did not become nationally important in the United States until well after the war, when it became clear that people would have to learn how to read if the nation was to become united through the power of the written word.

After the Revolutionary War, Americans' main concern was how to unify their new nation. While religion continued to be the dominating element in American education, patriotism had become almost equally as important. The last of the European-born settlers from before the revolution were starting to die off, leaving children who no longer felt strong ties to the way people did things in "the old country." More books and newspapers were being printed in the U.S., and fewer were being imported from Europe. Town governments were becoming stronger, and people were developing a deeper sense of community. All of these factors contributed to the growing feelings of unity and had two major effects on American education. First, it led to the development of standardized textbooks, and second, it led to the development of a public school system.

The Development of Standardized Textbooks

By the early 1800s, there were already a number of textbooks produced in the U.S. specifically for Americans. Noah Webster's *Blue-Backed Speller* helped standardize U.S. spelling and pronunciation, and millions of elementary school children used a series of six books called the *McGuffey Eclectic Readers* that combined a patriotic tone with somber religious morals. There was also

Dilworth's *New Guide to the Mother Tongue*, Colburn's *First Lessons on Arithmetic on the Plan of Pestalozzi*, and the ever-popular text entitled *A Grammatical Institute to the English Language Comprising an Easy, Concise, and Systematizing Method of Education, Designed for the English Schools of America.*

The problem with many of these early textbooks was the stereotypes they promoted by emphasizing the traits of "good Americans." They depicted good Americans as deeply religious (preferably Protestant), honest, thrifty, hardworking, and brave. Rural people were better than "citified" people because their characters were formed by nature and they weren't likely to be as smart-alecky as those city slickers. People of English, Scottish, German, and Swiss ancestry seemed to fit the definition perfectly, while anyone who had a different culture and beliefs, or even a different skin color or facial features, was described unfavorably. For example, these books often described American Indians as savages who could not be civilized and Spanish-speaking people as lazy and cruel.

Because the federal government didn't regulate school facilities until the early twentieth century, urban classrooms were often held in cramped and filthy industrial buildings like these abandoned and condemned warehouses.

The Development of a Public School System

Also in the early 1800s, it became clear that the old kinds of school funding were not going to work in the expanding country and that better ways were going to have to be devised to fund schools. Except for a few academies and free school societies, most schools in the U.S. had been controlled and supported by religious organizations. Many people in the United States began to feel that a country claiming that all of its citizens were created equal should have a system of *public* education — in other words, free, compulsory, tax-supported schools without religious controls. Others were enraged at the idea

The orphan trains: placing out in America

To many early colonists, particularly those who believed people were born evil, it was the purpose of education to thrash the evil out of children to save their souls. By the mid-1800s, that thinking had changed, and people came to see children as not only innocent but vulnerable to the evils of an industrial society.

The Orphan Trains were a successful system of charitable programs that operated from the 1850s to the 1920s to save children from these evils by resettling thousands of poor urban orphan children (like those shown here) with rural foster parents in the West. (Many of these children were orphans of first-generation immigrants from famine-plagued countries such as Ireland who died shortly after arriving in the U.S. Although most people assumed all those involved in the program were orphans, many of the children were separated from at least one living parent, and some of those "placed out" were poor adult women and not children at all.) These programs grew in response to two major nineteenth-century social dilemmas: the acute poverty and horrific living conditions caused by the urban industrial revolution in which children were working twelve to fifteen hours a day in mills, collecting rags, or simply begging in the streets just to stay alive; and the terrific lack of labor in western rural areas caused by the great westward

migrations. The newly developed railroads provided the fastest, cheapest way to address both problems.

Charles Loring Brace, a New York City reformer and the first to start a placing-out program, resettled over two hundred thousand urban children to country homes in the West by train. After a while, cities in the Midwest started to become urbanized, and they too instituted Orphan Train programs, shipping their orphans even further west to Montana and California. Brace's program (and the others) had widespread support by a public who believed them to be a noble and just cause. It was not until social changes in the 1920s caused people to start questioning the long-term effects of the system that these migrations stopped.

of paying school taxes, and some wanted to fight to keep religious control in the schools. Changes didn't exactly happen overnight.

Although most people gradually came to accept the need for public, tax-supported schools, not all states had begun establishing such a system before 1865. One factor that help speed up the process was the rapid population growth in the 1800s due to the waves of European and Asian immigrants. The schools were expected to contribute to these people's becoming "Americanized," not just because they would learn the language, but because they would be indoctrinated in U.S. patriotism and ideals by learning about the country's history, beliefs, and foundations.

There were certain religious groups such as the Roman Catholics and Lutherans who did not agree with the teaching methods or subjects taught in public schools and continued to offer private, parochial school educations. A number of wealthy people also preferred not to send their children to public schools, preferring expensive (and elite) private schools. But overall, a new awareness of education had taken hold.

The Age of the Common School, 1830-1865

The period from 1830 up to the Civil War is often called the Age of the Common School, because for the first time in U.S. history, its citizens were demanding a common education for (almost) everyone. Textbooks, blackboards, school buildings, the quality of teachers, the scope and depth of subject matter — all became important considerations in measuring the worth of an education.

In the East, the academy became the most important school of this period, replacing the old Latin grammar school and offering a broader curriculum, especially in practical subjects. In the frontier territories where settlers wanted their children to get out of school and pick up a trade rather than learn more than the three "Rs," the one-room country school continued to be the norm. In states that were already operating public elementary school systems, people were beginning to consider how to offer public education beyond that level.

Above and below: In the 1800s, anti-Chinese (and other) racist groups violently protested the use of public funds to educate minorities. Many people were even more outraged when public money was used to educate females, such as those in this high school science class.

Birth of the American High School

It would be hard to come up anything more "American" in U.S. cities and towns than the traditional public high school. In reality, however, high schools have been around only a relatively short time. When Boston opened the nation's first high school in 1821, it immediately stirred up intense national controversy. The people opposed to it were property owners who felt that if parents wanted their children to prepare for college and learn foreign languages, they should foot the bill themselves. They did not believe that secondary education should be available to everyone.

Although other high schools were established after 1821, these opponents did not legally challenge the use of public funds to support them until they took the case to the Michigan Supreme Court in 1874. They lost. The court ruled that local governments could use tax money to support secondary as well as elementary schools, a landmark decision that opened the way not just for public high schools throughout the country, but for public kindergartens, vocational schools, community colleges, technical institutes, and special education classes for the physically and intellectually challenged and for the gifted.

Opposition to public funding of schools did not stop, however, and public schools faced other serious roadblocks, including increasing racial tension and bigotry. Anti-Chinese groups (known as anti-coolie clubs), as well as the Ku Klux Klan and other racist vigilante groups, used violence and smear tactics to prevent non-white

minorities from attending schools supported by public funds. Educational changes for these minority groups — as well as for women and various immigrant groups — were slow to come.

How Education Changed for Women

In the first few decades of the nineteenth century, the New England bias against educating women — the feeling that learning housewifely duties was education enough — pervaded most of the nation's schools. Occasionally, if an academy teacher was hired to teach a certain number of pupils and fewer boys showed up than were originally planned, girls were allowed to fill their seats. As late as 1840, when the country's sixth census was taken, the statistics of women, like those of African-Americans and American Indians, were not considered in the counting of the number of citizens over the age of twenty who could read and write.

In 1841, women delegates were even excluded from participation in a World Anti-Slavery Convention, an action that finally enraged politically active women enough to form their own women's rights movement. It was not until 1875, however, that they began to have a significant impact on the nation's educational policies.

Important leaders in this growing women's movement included Catherine Beecher, Mary Lyon, Almira Phelps, and Emma Willard. Their combined efforts also helped establish the first coeducational college program at Oberlin, Ohio, in 1838. Twelve women's colleges were founded in 1880-1889, and by 1875, there were 311 separate girls-only schools in the United States.

Nineteenth-century pioneer in education Emma Hart Willard, one of the first to start an academy exclusively for the higher education of women. A teacher and author of both textbooks and poetry, she spent over fifty years working for educational equality.

A Georgia law passed in 1829

And be it further enacted that if any slave, negro or free person of colour or any white person shall teach any other slave, negro, or free person of colour, to read or write either written or printed characters, the said free person of colour, or slave, shall be punished by fine and whipping, or fine or whipping at the discretion of the court; and if a white person so offending, he, she, or they shall be punished with fine, not exceeding five hundred dollars, and imprisonment, in the common jail at the discretion of the court before whom said offender is tried.

Education of African-Americans in the 1800s

Susie King Taylor, an African-American writer who was born under a Georgia slave law that made it illegal to educate Blacks, wrote an eloquent account of her secret, passionate efforts to gain an education in spite of that law. When she was ten, her mother secretly sent Susie and her brother each day to a "clandestine" school held in the home of a free Black widow on the other side of town. They had to wrap their books in newspaper to conceal them from police and other potentially hostile white people. The thirty children in Mrs. Woodhouse's school were careful to show up one or two at a time, entering her kitchen yard through the back gate. Neighbors were not suspicious as long as they believed she was just teaching a few children a trade, such as sewing.

Susie studied reading and writing so enthusiastically in Mrs. Woodhouse's kitchen classroom that in two years she had learned everything the widow could teach her. After that, she continued to take advantage of every opportunity to learn. At first she persuaded a white friend named Katie O'Connor to teach her the arithmetic and history lessons she was learning in school. Susie also read everything she could get her hands on, from novels to political pamphlets to religious scripture. And she started to keep a journal, a careful documentary of what it was like to grow up female and Black in the pre-Civil War South.

Susie's story is not an unusual one. The harsh laws passed by Southern states in the early 1800s did not stop the ingenious efforts of slaves and Black freemen to acquire an education for themselves and their children. A white woman named Margaret Douglas served a month in the Norfolk, Virginia, jail for the "crime" of teaching Sunday school to slave children. She was not the only white person to break this law. Many southerners, both white and Black, held secret "clandestine" schools in their kitchens and attics, some teaching African-Americans the basics of reading and writing.

African Free School

NOTICE

Parents and Guardians of Coloured Children are hereby informed, that a Male and Female School has long been established for coloured children, by the Manumission Society of New York where pupils receive such an education as is calculated to fit them for usefulness and respectability. The male school is situated in Mulberry Street, to which is attached a female school; all are under the management of experienced teachers. The boys are taught Reading, Writing, Arithmetic, Geography and English Grammar — and the Girls, in addition to those branches, are taught Sewing, Marking, and Knitting, etc.

Pupils of 5 to fifteen years of age are admitted by the Teachers of the School, at the rate of twenty-five cents to one dollar per quarter according to the circumstances of the parents; and the children of such as cannot afford to pay anything are admitted free of expense and enjoy the same advantages as those who pay.

— Advertisement in *The Rights of All,* Volume 1, No.1 (May 29, 1829), p. 8

Attitudes toward the education of African-Americans changed about 1830 as the tensions mounted that would break out in the Civil War. As northerners (both white and Black) became increasingly militant in their demands for the abolition of slavery, slave owners, especially in the South, became more afraid of slave revolts. And they believed that educating their slaves increased the danger of that revolt.

Elementary education was available to free Blacks in the North in privately run schools, but as the public school system developed and the controversy over slavery grew, whites could not come to any clear agreement on whether or not to include African-American students in the public schools. The policy that was eventually adopted would strongly affect African-American education for the next hundred years. Although the decision was bitterly opposed by African-American families in Massachusetts at the time, the Supreme Court of Massachusetts made a landmark decision in 1849 when it ruled in *Boston v. Roberts* for the establishment of segregated public schools. By 1857, Massachusetts passed a law *banning* segregation, but much damage had already been done by the earlier ruling in favor of segregation. This ruling not only set the precedent for school segregation, but it shows how even in the more liberal North, the issue of African-American education often came up against much bigotry and resentment. Segregation was also not the only issue. There was also controversy over what *kind* of education Blacks should receive — if they needed to learn anything beyond basic reading skills and a trade. The African-American drive for education was just as passionate as its drive for freedom. Anyone who learned to read felt an obligation to teach others their skills.

Booker T. Washington advocated training African-Americans for trades to build up their economic position before fighting for integration and equality. This strategy was opposed by more militant Black leaders, such as W. E. B. Du Bois.

It is estimated that by 1860, there were about four thousand African-Americans enrolled in schools in the slave states and about twenty-three thousand enrolled in the free states. Only twenty-eight African-American college graduates were recorded before the Civil War, and the literacy rate among African-Americans in 1866 was estimated to be only 10 percent. Missionaries and northern abolitionists contributed both funds and teachers to the effort to educate Blacks. Their work would not have had much of an impact, however, without the support of the federal government. During the Civil War, the newly created Freedmen's Bureau joined forces with the various missionary and support groups working for African-American education and built over four thousand schools to teach everyone in Black communities from small children to grandparents. In spite of their efforts, however, Black education remained inferior in quality to the education being offered to whites at that time. In addition, the segregated freedmen's schools emphasized "industrial" education and offered very few liberal arts subjects.

The Catholic school alternative

Catholic schools were controversial in U.S. history right from the start. Early in colonial days, the few Catholics in America were suspected and feared and pretty much lived their lives outside the cultural and political activities of the community. There were rigid laws during the Revolutionary era that restricted the freedom of Catholics to worship, participate in public life, and educate their children. The thoroughly Protestant schools used Protestant textbooks that were filled with derogatory remarks about Catholics. (For example, a text called the *New English Tutor* showed a picture of the Pope with the caption, "Child, behold the Man of Sin, the Pope, worthy of thy utmost hatred!")

By 1850, there were only 1.6 million Catholics in the U.S., but that small community fought hard to change the educational situation. They demanded that offensive passages be deleted from school textbooks, asked that Catholic children be excused from the daily Protestant school prayers, and requested that a portion of school tax money be given to the Catholic community to help support separate Catholic schools. They would continue to fight for the last issue well into the twentieth century, long after Protestant control of the public schools had faded. For most Americans, the issue of whether or not Catholics sent their children to separate, nonpublic schools was no problem as long as Catholic parents paid for these schools. It continues to be a controversy even today in areas where religious and other private groups are asking for a share of community taxes to support their schools.

tem.) Special "camp" schools were started that actually followed mining, logging, and railroad crews as they moved from place to place.

The nation's traditional public school system also underwent some radical changes to accommodate the tremendous influx of new students. The first step in most areas was a quick and massive building program. "Steamer" classes (named after the ships on which most immigrants sailed to America) gave non-English-speaking immigrant children six months to learn their new language before entering regular public school classes. (Before steamer classes were introduced, all non-English-speaking immigrant children were forced to enter school at the first-grade level, regardless of their age.)

New subjects such as domestic science (now called home economics) and physical education were introduced to meet the needs of the immigrant poor. Teaching foreign-born girls American housekeeping and cooking skills was supposed to improve nutrition and money management in immigrant households. Physical education courses were designed to offer slum children an alternative to playing on the streets — and to teach kids all-American sports like baseball. Public schools also took over more of a social service role by offering children medical examinations and health care.

Perhaps one of the most successful ideas in early twentieth century education was the introduction of school lunches. In New York City, for example, a private organization called the School Lunch Committee began to offer penny lunches that were carefully designed to suit the ethnic tastes of each separate neighborhood. Because most immigrant mothers were forced to work outside the home, few children could go home for lunch and ended up spending the few pennies they had from the junk food carts that always

The Chinese not only faced much more prejudice and stereotyping than white, Northern European immigrants, but many also found it harder to learn the language.

surrounded the school. School lunches were a nutritious and popular alternative, and they soon caught on throughout the U.S.

Providing education for the country's new immigrants caused a great deal of controversy. Many people believed that all Americans should be raised under the value system of the dominant European-American, English-speaking, middle-class, Protestant majority. Some of these people started a movement that demanded that all children be required to attend public schools.

The Americanization Movement

In 1914, with the outbreak of World War I, native-born Americans suddenly discovered a whole new dimension to their immigrant problem: national security. Cultural diversity now came to mean disloyalty to the U.S. government. Immigrants who kept their old language and customs might be conspiring to commit treason. This war hysteria grew to such proportions that the "foreign element" in larger cities

Learning the *American* way *to* make a birdhouse or a cake.

Educating Mexican-Americans to be farm workers

After the start of the Mexican Revolution in 1910, thousands of Mexican peasants were forced by inflation, extreme poverty, and the horrors of war to migrate to El Norte, as they called the Southwest U.S. In the early twentieth century, U.S.citizens encouraged Mexicans to migrate. Their labor was needed, not just in the cotton and beet fields, but in the development of the growing railroad network. About 25,000 Mexicans crossed the border during the first decade, and another 170,000 crossed between 1910 and 1920. Most settled in Texas, Arizona, New Mexico, and California, and they soon found themselves trapped in unskilled blue-collar and agricultural jobs.

While these immigrants were welcomed with open arms into the U.S. work force, they were definitely not welcomed socially. They were expected to assume a respectful body posture and tone of voice in the presence of Anglos. They were permitted to shop in the Anglo business sections of most southwestern towns only on Saturdays, and while they were allowed to patronize Anglo cafes, they were only allowed to sit at the counters. (Some restaurants even preferred losing business to serving Mexicans and put signs in their windows stating "No dogs or Mexicans.")

When it came to education, the racism was even stronger. Growers in Texas and the Southwest were only interested in educating Mexican-American children to take the places of their parents as agricultural laborers. These growers had a great deal of influence on local politics, which in turn dictated how schools

were run. A Texas school superintendent whose job it was to enforce the state's compulsory school attendance law, explained why he didn't apply the law to Mexican-American students: "If a man has very much sense or education either, he is not going to stick to this kind of work. So you see it is up to the white population to keep the Mexican on his knees in an onion patch."

Most Mexican-American children who did go to school in the early 1900s attended segregated schools with a curriculum that emphasized housekeeping skills and manual training. Teachers also made sure their Mexican-American students were taught the appropriate attitudes of hard work and disciplined behavior. As one Los Angeles teacher put it, "Mexican boys and girls must keep in mind that employees must be pliant, obedient, courteous, and willing to help their employer's enterprise." Most children were advised not to plan on attending school past the sixth grade.

But Mexican-American parents had no intention of having their children confined to lives of picking beets or digging ditches. Even those who barely earned enough to feed their families did everything they could to keep their children in school for as long as they possibly could. Many did this gladly, even when it meant creating a cultural distance between themselves and their children. The Catholic church, a strong factor in the Mexican-American community, often took an active interest in educating Mexican-Americans, and those who could afford the tuition often sent their children to private Catholic schools.

was soon considered a national menace. In 1916, when Theodore Roosevelt was running for president, he actually announced that he wanted no one's support unless that person was "prepared to say that every citizen of this country has got to be pro United States first, last, and all the time, and not pro anything else at all." Anything less, he said, including any ethnic tie, was "moral treason."

By 1921, more than thirty states had "Americanization" laws. Thousands of school systems throughout the U.S. organized English and civics classes for the foreign born. So did local Chambers of Commerce, unions, patriotic organizations, and even the federal government. The problem was that there was no organization to the effort.

Teaching those immigrants to cook *American* food

Loyalty to America was no longer enough. The Americanizers demanded loyalty to the *American way of life.* That meant adopting the habits, practices, and virtues of the white, Anglo-Saxon, Protestant middle class. Anything less, no matter how trivial the issue, was not true loyalty. To become a U.S. citizen, an immigrant had to learn the American way to brush her teeth, clean his fingernails, air out the family bedding, prepare baby food, and wash clothes. Not only were these topics (and more!) the subject of endless manuals immigrants were supposed to study, but naturalization classes actually made them act these out in class-room drills. The General Federation of Women's Clubs, for example, launched a vigorous campaign against cabbage. One of the most important things immigrant women must be taught, they believed, was how to cook American vegetables instead of that awful European cabbage.

Although great numbers of immigrants enrolled in the Americanization programs between 1914 and 1925, over three-quarters of them never completed them. The Americanizers wanted to transform every immigrant into a 100 percent English-speaking American. This was a grandiose expectation of a group of people who had to work twelve to fifteen hours every day and then struggle to raise their families in a filthy slum.

It wasn't until the late 1920s, after federal laws had begun to restrict the number of annual immigrants, that the enthusiasm for the melting-pot idea finally began to change. It would take until the 1960s for the change to take full effect, but many Americans were starting to see that it was their common ideals and goals — and the *diversity* of America's people, not their sameness — that gave the country its strength.

The Rise of Progressive Education

The most obvious feature of U.S. education in the twentieth century is the tremendous growth in the numbers of students, teachers, and school buildings at all levels of learning. Secondary education grew in this period, just as elementary education had done in the previous century, until high school became standard for almost all children. With more and more money spent building new schools, training more teachers, and developing new teaching materials, education has become big business in this century. This century has also seen some amazing technological advances in teaching, including highly specialized industrial training, public and private early childhood education, and sophisticated teaching methods using computers, television, and video.

Along with these changes came significant changes in how the U.S. saw education's responsibility to society. The teaching methods of the 1800s stressed memorization and discipline. At the turn of the century, the goal of most educational leaders was to blend all Americans (especially immigrants) into a national community. But by 1900, many educators felt that the schools were not keeping up with the changes in society and suggested that education should focus more on the growth of the child. The educational movement that grew out of this new belief was called Progressive Education.

The Progressive Educational movement in the U.S. was an association of private, experimental schools that developed throughout the country between 1919 and 1950. Although they were eventually phased out, the philosophy upon which they were founded had a profound effect on many public schools in this country as well.

Basically, teachers who promoted Progressive education believed that education's primary goal was the complete development of every child. They felt that teaching methods such as field trips, group discussions, and creative activities would help children prepare for life in a democracy. They believed that the basic three "Rs" of reading, writing, and arithmetic should be broadened for all students to include geography, history, and science. The teachers' role was to be guide, not disciplinarian, and their job was to make the subject matter as interesting as possible for their students. Each student was given the freedom to develop according to his or her own interests, with a curriculum that also included nature study, music, handicrafts, field geography, drama, storytelling, games, and number concepts.

Greater attention was also given to each child's health and physical development. Some of the better, more lasting influences of Progressive education movement include better lighting and air ventilation in the classrooms, safe playgrounds, and promoting physical exercise and sports for fitness. Progressive education also placed a greater emphasis on the role of parents in determining school policy.

But many educational experiments conducted in the name of Progressive education failed over the years, too — experiments with different curriculums, little classroom discipline, strange new ideas of how to teach reading and math, and classes in behavioral and emotional adjustment. By the early 1950s, when the United States was competing with the Soviet Union for economic and political domination of the world, Americans began to take a long, critical look at public education. Many didn't like what they saw. They believed that Soviet schools were giving children a better education, and that the Progressive movement was to blame. Studies were done and recommendations were made, and as a result, the 1950s and 1960s saw a great deal of educational reform.

Federal Aid and Educational Reform After WWII

Learning in the U.S. went through a number of dramatic changes after the end of World War II. The postwar baby boom led to higher school enrollments in the early 1950s, which led to the need for more schools. And with the need for more schools came the need for more money to build and run the schools. As a result, federal school aid also had to be increased. Congress passed a number of laws to aid education during the mid-1900s. These included the

G.I. Bill (which granted federal money to armed forces personnel for college education upon leaving the military) and several bills in the fifties, sixties, and seventies that also made money available for higher education and gave financial aid to local school districts.

In the 1970s, after the peak of the baby boom had passed, school enrollment began to decline. As a result, many of the schools built in the fifties and sixties were closed. Federal aid to education also declined, and these cuts in funding caused additional schools to either close or cut back on the services they offered.

After World War II and the wars in Korea and Vietnam, U.S. classrooms saw a growing influx of Korean, Chinese, Hmong, Thai, Laotian, Vietnamese, and other Asian-born immigrant children.

As we shall see in the next chapter, declining enrollment and reduction in federal aid to schools are just a few of the challenges U.S. schools have faced in their efforts to guarantee equal educational opportunities to all, including women and minorities. The years following World War II have brought with them the challenge of educating new waves of immigrants. While progress has been made in the past several decades in the struggle for equal rights and equal educational opportunities for minorities, many Puerto Rican, Cuban, Haitian, Mexican, Korean, Hmong, Thai, and numerous other immigrant children and their parents still suffer discrimination and inequality. Most educators now appreciate the tremendous wealth of this country's cultural diversity, and many challenges remain in trying to figure out the best way to put that diversity to use in the nation's classrooms.

Teachers' organizations in the mid-1900s also became more militant as they bargained for better salaries and increased benefits. The strikes they waged in the 1960s and early 1970s were successful. They increased teachers' annual salaries during that time by an average of 70 percent.

African-Americans Lead the Battle Against School Discrimination in the Twentieth Century

The passion Blacks had for education in pre-Civil War days burned even brighter after they had won their freedom. After the war, the Freedman's Bureau, which was under the War Department, joined forces with missionary groups and various aid societies to organize over four thousand schools for former slaves. In spite of these efforts, however, education for African-Americans remained inferior to that available to whites, especially in the South. For one thing, the schools were segregated. For another, the public schools set up for African-Americans in the Reconstruction period were of much lower quality than those attended by whites.

Louisiana, 1939. No matter how poor or oppressed, African-American parents did everything possible to make sure their children got at least a basic education, even if that meant teaching them at home.

It was in this post-Civil War atmosphere that the demand for racial equality in education really began to grow. Some Black leaders, like Booker T. Washington, a leading African-American educator, argued for compromise, diplomacy, and working within the system. Others, such as W. E. B. Du Bois, a brilliant Harvard Ph.D., insisted that protest and struggle were the only means by which African-Americans could ever hope to achieve educational, social, or political equality. At first, Washington had greater influence in the Black community, but in 1905, Du Bois founded the Niagara Movement in African-American education. Not only were changes in Black education slow in coming, but in 1908, Kentucky upheld a law that made separate instruction for Blacks and whites mandatory.

In the next year, 1909, members of the Niagara Movement joined with Du Bois to found the National Association for the Advancement of Colored People (NAACP), a voice for social as well as educational change. The NAACP gathered evidence to prove the inequality of education for African-Americans and convince people that the separate facilities should be made absolutely equal or abolished altogether. They started to meet with some success. In 1938, for example, the Supreme Court ordered that Missouri build a Black law school equal to the one that existed in that state for whites — or admit a Black student who had applied to the University of Missouri. Obviously, it was cheaper for the state to admit the student, yet there was so much horror and opposition to this idea on the part of many whites that other states (Oklahoma, for example) actually built a new Black law school rather than admit African-Americans into its white law schools. Many other people (who had once honestly believed separate-but-equal facilities could work just fine) now began to see the absurdity of separate schools. They were ready to accept integration.

Throughout the 1930s and 1940s, with the rise of labor unions and Depression-bred social reformers, African-Americans were becoming more and more vocal about the issues of desegregation and educational equality. It finally came to a crisis in 1954, when the U.S. Supreme Court (in *Brown v. the Board of Education of Topeka*) finally ruled that "separate educational facilities are inherently unequal," and ordered that the country's schools be integrated "with all deliberate speed." The dream of equality voiced by such historic African-American leaders as Nat Turner, Frederick Douglass, Harriet Tubman, W. E. B. Du Bois, and, in modern times, Martin Luther King, Jr., was finally beginning to take shape.

The African-American drive for equality picked up momentum in the fifties and sixties. There were boycotts, Freedom Rides, sit-ins at lunch counters, and voter registration drives. There was the 1963 March on Washington. While *de jure* segregation was finally outlawed (that is, white and Black schools kept separate by state and local laws), *de facto* segregation (neighborhood schools being all Black or all white because the neighborhoods were segregated) was still very real — and not just in the South. The goal was no longer equal access — the equal right to enroll in a school or sit in a classroom. It now became equal results — a demand for materials and programs that would close the gaps in educational achievement, and a demand for an accurate portrayal of African-American history in the country's history books. While the *Brown* decision certainly did breathe new life into the energy and dreams of this country's oppressed minorities, few in the fifties fully realized the long haul that lay ahead.

In the early 1960s, many whites and Blacks alike became Freedom Riders who traveled in the South to check on the progress of racial desegregation. Others staged sit-in demonstrations at lunch counters and other segregated public facilities. Many of these people met with white mob violence in their fight for racial equality.

Busing and the Quest for Racial Balance

While considerable progress was made desegregating U.S. schools in the late fifties and sixties, *de facto* segregation remained a problem in many school districts, even in the North, where inner-city populations were often all Black, while students in a more affluent, suburban neighborhood school may have been all white.

Busing groups of Black students to predominantly white schools and white students to Black schools became one of the solutions to this type of segregation. It was a controversial solution. Many parents (white and Black)

objected to having their elementary school children attend schools other than those in their own neighborhoods. Some parents whose children were bused into urban schools were afraid it would introduce their children to foul language, crime, and drugs, while both African- and European-American parents of high school students were concerned that long daily bus rides would prevent their children from going out for extracurricular sports and club activities scheduled after school hours. Racist European-American parents who had moved their families to all-white suburbs for the express purpose of avoiding integrated schools were particularly upset. As a result, in many communities throughout the U.S., efforts to bus students to achieve racial balance in the schools met with bitter and often violent opposition.

Busing became so controversial an issue that the U.S. government finally stepped in. The Civil Rights Act, passed by Congress in 1964, not only specified that no person could be discriminated against on the basis of race, color, sex,

Top: Boston inner-city children register for a 1965 busing program out of Roxbury to less crowded, previously all-white schools. They were met with violence that surprised those who thought racial hatred was strictly a product of the South.
Bottom: Racial integration became a reality for these Washington, D.C., kids when their classes started in 1954-55.

or national origin in any program that received federal assistance, it threatened to withhold that assistance from any school districts or states that failed to institute reasonable plans for integration. In 1971, the Supreme Court took an even more specific stand on the issue of school busing. In the case of *Swann v. the Charlotte-Mecklenburg Board of Education*, it held that busing is indeed a constitutionally acceptable method of integrating schools.

In spite of these efforts to uphold the practice of busing, however, militant resistance to busing did not die out. In 1974, riots over the busing of Black students to South Boston High School were so violent the schools had to be closed. In many cities today, school systems comply with the court order through magnet schools, which specialize in certain subjects, such as science, math, art, or foreign languages. These specialty schools attract students from various urban and suburban neighborhoods, thus encouraging integration through voluntary means.

American Indians Struggle for Equality

American Indians also became more vocal in their struggle for equality in the twentieth century. A Pan-Indian movement was officially started with the founding of the Society of American Indians in Columbus, Ohio, in 1911. From its founding until 1923, the society provided a meeting ground for the most progressive, reform-minded Indians in the country, including Dr. Charles A. Eastman, a Santee Sioux who graduated with a medical degree from Dartmouth; Charles E. Daganett, a part-Peoria Indian who played an important role in the Bureau of Indian Affairs; Henry Roe Cloud, a Winnebago who was Yale University's first Indian graduate; and Angel Decora, a talented Winnebago artist who worked hard for Indian rights and influenced the direction of new Indian art.

For years, they lobbied without success for a "National Indian Day," supported Indian athletes such as Olympic champion Jim Thorpe, and worked hard to change the national stereotypes that depicted Indians as wild savages. While the society was greatly concerned with educational reform and the worsening health and housing conditions among Native Americans, the group's preoccupation with internal disputes diminished its effectiveness. Perhaps their most vocal stand was on the issue of keeping Indian soldiers segregated during World War I. American Indians were among the first minority groups to volunteer for military service, their proud warrior tradition and sense of loyalty winning out over whatever resentments they held toward the U.S. government. On the home front, another ten thousand Indian women and men became Red Cross workers. Despite the intensity of their wartime sacrifices, however, Indians still did not have the right to vote after World War I. They didn't get it until 1924, when Congress finally passed the Indian Citizenship Act.

Indian participation in World War II and the Korean War was even more commendable. Twenty-five thousand Indians joined the Navy, Army, or Marine Corps, and another forty thousand between the ages of eighteen and fifty worked in the war-support industry at home. Sadly, these people did not get a hero's welcome upon their return. In some states (Arizona and New Mexico, for example) they were still not allowed to vote, and they were denied the loans and educational privileges other G.I.s qualified for. A National Congress of American Indians had been created in 1944 to address Indian grievances against the government, but by 1963, only 122 of the 588 claims originally filed were even processed. In 1950, Dillon Meyer was named the Commissioner of Indian Affairs, and his first efforts were aimed at "freeing" Indians from the nation's reservation system as soon as possible. He called it "Termination." Unfortunately, his vision of how to accomplish this was to Americanize Indians

An American Indian G.I. visits his family while on leave during World War II (above), and a group of Seminoles cast their first U.S. votes (below). Although Indians have had an outstanding record of courageous military service in every twentieth-century U.S. war, they were not even allowed to vote until 1924. After WWII, many states also denied them loans and educational benefits.

In the 1950s, the public still didn't know what to do about the "problem" of educating American Indian children. Here, Navajo children are taught the "Three Rs" in a cramped reservation school trailer.

so they could be "mainstreamed" into U.S. society. By 1957, almost fifteen thousand Indians were "relocated" to city jobs, apartments, and schools. For many, this meant yet one more forced removal in a series of forced — and traumatic — dislocations. The 1960 Census counted 525,000 Native Americans as "urban Indians." Of these, thousands faced the loneliness, alcoholism, depression, police harassment, unemployment, and crime of city life without any preparation or governmental support.

While Indians as a minority group benefited from the African-American struggles for equality in the 1950s and 1960s, in the 1980s, the Reagan administration undermined many gains that Indians may have made. The special Senate hearings on Indian Affairs of 1988 and 1989 proved to be nothing but empty talk. In the next chapter, we'll take a closer look at the demands Indians have made for educational changes today.

The Reagan years — A step backward for American Indians?

When interviewed as a presidential candidate, Ronald Reagan unwittingly confessed to his disregard for American Indians by declaring that he was "fascinated by this new world — Cortés, Lewis and Clark, Father Serra — when it was still virtually untouched by man." Later, when asked by a student how the U.S. could possibly justify its Indian policy over the years, Reagan was quoted as saying, "Maybe we made a mistake in trying to maintain Indian cultures. Maybe we should not have humored them in wanting to stay in that primitive kind of life style. Maybe we should have said, 'No, come join us. Be citizens along with the rest of us.'" It was a clear sign of how little empathy or understanding the nation had of the Indian struggles for equality, their level of poverty, or the discrimination they faced in public schools, even at the top level of its leadership. Some Indian leaders feel that the Reagan presidency was the worst administration for the rights of Indians since the days of outright warfare and termination.

Women's Educational Advances

The twentieth century was also a time of change in education for women. In some cases, women benefited from the advancement of other causes — the improvement of school buildings and curriculum during the Progressive era and the passing of child labor laws, for example. But the cause of female education itself did not advance at a steady rate throughout the U.S. By 1902, some states offered coeducational opportunities to women while some staunchly did not. While all women faced discrimination because of sex (they weren't even allowed to vote until the Nineteenth Amendment was passed in 1920), minority women, especially Hispanic and African-American women, faced racial prejudice as well.

While winning the right to vote in 1920 was a major victory for women in the U.S., it was sadly one of the last real gains the movement made until World War II, when many men went overseas to fight. Women all over the nation ably stepped in to fill the roles formerly given to men, yet once the men returned, women were again treated as second-class citizens.

It was not until the 1960s that U.S. women finally began to experience significant changes. Educational as well as social and economic issues finally received national attention in 1961. This was the year that saw both the birth of the President's Commission on the Status of Women and a follow-up drive by the National Federation of Business and Professional Women's Clubs. Equally important was the publication in 1963 of Betty Friedan's *The Feminine Mystique*, a book that established its author as one of the most visible leaders of the women's movement. In 1964 and 1965, Congress passed two laws that helped advance women's education by authorizing money for adult education. In October 1966, the women's movement really began to pick up momentum with the founding of the National Organization for Women (NOW) and the Women's Equity Action League (WEAL).

One of the most powerful statements for equality in education was the passage of the Education Amendment to the 1972 Equal Employment Opportunity Act. It stated that "No person in the United States shall, on the basis of sex, be excluded from participation in, be denied the benefits of, or be subjected to discrimination under any education program or activity receiving Federal assistance." In the next chapter, we'll see what more has been done to resist the subtle forms of sexism and discrimination in our schools.

Educating Exceptional Children in the Twentieth Century

American Indians held the belief that the gods had a special concern for children born with disabilities and that it was everyone's job to share that special concern. Throughout the rest of the world, however, the attitude toward people with disabilities has historically been one of rejection. By the 1800s, some small efforts were being made in Europe and the United States to educate people with disabilities, although the prejudice against them was clear enough in the accepted vocabulary used to describe them — words like "deaf and dumb," "feeble-minded," and "idiot." Thomas Gallaudet's work training teachers for deaf students in Connecticut won him worldwide recognition. John Fisher took the techniques he had learned in Paris to teach people with disabilities and established the New England Asylum for the Blind, whose students went on to inspire the parents of disabled children around the world. Inspiring as their achievements were, however, their approaches all had one factor in common: that of isolating people with disabilities from the rest of society. It was not until 1871, when a day school was established for deaf students in Boston, that it was at least possible for disabled children to still live at home with their families.

Above: Elizabeth Farrell (third from the left in front row) brought her fight for the education of exceptional children to international attention at world education councils held in Washington, D.C.

Two young schoolmates carry on a conversation at recess. One is from a regular-education program, the other from an exceptional-education program. But thanks to their school's "mainstream" integration program, they share many of the same educational experiences.

One of the most effective spokespersons for this new concept of *not* keeping disabled students out of the mainstream was Alexander Graham Bell, a noted speech expert as well as a celebrated inventor. At the 1898 convention of the National Education Association, he proposed that people with special needs should be educated in public schools by specially trained teachers. He knew only too well that this innovative concept would require money, and when it became clear that his new invention, the telephone, would make him quite rich, he wrote his mother, saying, "Now we shall have money enough to teach speech to little deaf children."

Elizabeth Farrell and the Council for Exceptional Children

Not too long after the turn of the century, another remarkable person changed the scope of special education. Elizabeth Farrell, a young public school teacher in New York City, believed that disabled children should not be viewed as a group of unfortunates but should be treated instead as individuals, each given a chance to develop according to his or her full capabilities. School, she said, should adapt to them, and not the other way around. She organized classes for children with special physical, intellectual, and behavioral needs, and she even worked with groups of especially bright or gifted children.

In 1922, her work led her to organize what is now the Council for Exceptional Children. Her work has also led to the development of better testing and evaluation procedures, espe-

Christopher Nolan and computer technology

People with disabilities have been tremendously aided by advances in computer technology. Computerized voice recognition allows paralyzed people to dial a telephone, turn lights and electronic equipment off and on, even to write checks and compose letters. Optical character recognition computers and "talking" computers enable visually impaired people to access data banks, and computers attached to video cameras can even translate a person's eye movements into speech. Christopher Nolan, an Irish writer, is one of the best-known technological success stories. Nolan has not been able to walk, talk, or chew food since his birth in 1965 with a severe neurological disorder, and although he has no control over his arm or neck muscles, he has written a best-selling and critically praised book of poems and short stories (*Dam-Burst of Dreams*) and an autobiographical novel (*Under the Eye of the Clock*).

cially for minority groups, to determine the special educational needs of challenged children.

After WWII, programs for people with physical and developmental disabilities were expanded in almost all public schools to provide vocational rehabilitation and counseling. It was not until the 1970s, however, that significant gains were made for children with intellectual, emotional, behavioral, and learning disabilities. The most important government legislation for disabled children (regardless of their condition) is the Education for All Handicapped Children Act passed in 1975. Under this law, every disabled or gifted child is an exceptional child who is guaranteed not only a free public education but an education tailored to his or her special needs. The bill outlines the specifics of treatment and care of exceptional children, as well as methods of keeping track of their educational progress.

There is still some controversy over methods and funding for special education. But special education has now finally passed the stage where it is thought of as charity or even as something an enlightened society should find it in its conscience to do. In the 1971 landmark case of *Pennsylvania Association for the Retarded v. the Commonwealth of Pennsylvania*, the Supreme Court upheld the ruling that public schools could not violate a child's civil rights by ignoring his or her special educational needs.

The Road to Progress Stretches On

Both public and private schools made important changes in the early twentieth century. In reality, though, schools did little to promote social integration because little attention was given to the educational needs of children from non-white, non-middle-class backgrounds. Much has changed since World War II, thanks in part to the civil cights, Black Power, and women's movements, as well as to advocates for people with disabilities. But the nation's educational system still had a way to go. Today, multicultural education recognizes — and teaches us about — the tremendous variety in the American historical and cultural personality. And so the integration of people of various backgrounds and abilities may yet become a reality.

A group of students of various backgrounds and abilities collaborate on a number of projects in this modern, integrated classroom.

CHAPTER FOUR

Education Today: Kids and Multiculturalism

J oseph Young sits behind the wheel of his automobile on a bright Albuquerque May morning and watches his young son Frank cross the busy junior high school grounds, his trumpet case under one arm and his book bag slung over his shoulder, and he forgets for a moment that he is already running late for work. Instead, he watches his son disappear into the schoolyard and thinks back to his own childhood and what school was like for him.

Joe Young was raised in a traditional Navajo family on a New Mexico reservation, a family so poor that he and his brothers often had to hunt game to make sure the family had enough to eat. When he was six and his parents sent him to an Indian boarding school in Colorado, it was not just for an education but to make sure he ate regularly. Joe was a bright child, yet he had a hard time in school. Because he only returned home for just a few short weeks each year, he missed his tribe and family terribly. The teachers and staff of the school forced him to give up his tribal customs and beliefs, to cut his hair, and even adopt a new, "white" name. And he remembered the contempt many of his teachers had for his beliefs about nature and spirituality. Joe Young remembered how his teachers taught that North America was "discovered" by white European explorers. They lumped all Native American cultures together under the heading of "Indians," never mentioning the hundreds of years of their history and culture prior to the European invasions, trivializing their spiritual beliefs and cultural contributions. Despite feeling alienated and humiliated throughout much of his school years, Joe had an intense curiosity about science and mathematics and worked hard in school. He went on to attend the University of New Mexico on a tribal scholarship, where he studied nuclear physics. Although he is now one of the country's leading scientists, Joe Young still feels alienated by much of the European-American society in which he lives and works.

But as he watches Frank joking with his classmates that morning, classmates that include African-, European-, Hispanic-, and Asian-American kids, Joe Young feels good. His son is a popular student who works hard in class, gets good grades, and enjoys playing football and soccer. Proud of his Navajo heritage, Frank is an active member of the school's Navajo club, and he works hard to make sure his teachers include more Navajo history and literature in the school curriculum. He is also the president of his school's environmental protection club and has organized some pretty impressive recycling drives. Frank's current project is to convince his classmates to boycott two local fast-food restaurants that are still packaging their burgers in non-recyclable styrofoam.

Joe Young knows schools are still far from perfect. Too many of his children's classmates will drop out before they graduate high school, many because they will feel that school just doesn't offer them the technical skills they'll need to get good jobs. Some of Frank's friends resent a school system that makes them spend so much time on buses getting to and from school that they no longer have the chance to participate in sports and other after-school activities, like science club. Drugs and violence are major problems in schools all over the country, no matter what the ethnic makeup of the community or how rich or poor its inhabitants. Frank's school is no exception. The school board is still hotly debating how to keep guns off of school grounds without turning the school into a police state. While there is certainly more equality in U.S. schools than ever before, Joe knows that his daughter Sonia will have to fight harder to overcome the subtle (and sometimes not-so-subtle) gender discrimination that is still a problem in today's classrooms. The multicultural focus of schools does help reduce racism, but violence and bigotry still make headlines each day, both in school and out. He knows there's still a long way to go, and a lot of disagreement on how to get there.

Suddenly the bell rings and the kids start heading for the front doors. Remembering his own challenges for the day, Joe Young looks in the rear-view mirror and pulls his car away from the curb as he heads for work. His thoughts soon became absorbed in setting up his department's new energy experiments.

Schools Develop a Multicultural Awareness

The civil rights movement that gained momentum in the 1950s and 1960s called attention to the discrimination that many ethnic minorities confronted in U.S. schools. African-Americans were the first to demand equality, but Latino and American Indian groups soon followed. A big part of this movement was pride in ethnic culture — not

American students learn about Japanese Buddhist celebrations in the annual Bon Odori Festival of the Lanterns. On the second Saturday of each July, many Japanese-Americans don traditional kimonos and participate in an outdoor dance to the beat of traditional Taiko drums.

just each culture's distinctive history, but its language, art, and food and its contributions to entertainment and sports. As schools began offering courses and programs in cultural awareness, textbooks began to be rewritten to reflect more than just the middle-class Anglo, Protestant perspective that has for so long dominated studies of U.S. history and culture. Community and professional groups also began promoting cultural awareness programs on the level of adult education. Many communities fought the changes, but throughout the U.S. a new, multicultural focus was already beginning to dissolve old stereotypes and prejudices.

By the 1970s, many people agreed that the goals of U.S. schools should be to foster the intellectual, social, and personal development of students to their highest individual potential — and to provide *each* student, regardless of ethnic, social, or economic background, with an equal opportunity to learn.

They also came to understand another factor that has an important impact on how children learn: poverty. It is estimated that over 20 percent of school-age children in the U.S. live below the poverty level. About half of this group are minorities; half are white. Regardless of race, these students are statistically much more likely to drop out of school or to be expelled before they graduate high school. Most of those who do remain in school are achieving well below their potential. One of the ways many schools are helping to address this serious educational problem is to fortify children physically by offering free breakfast and lunch programs to poor and often malnourished children.

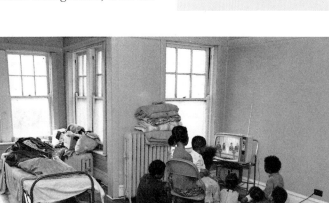

A life of poverty can have a dramatic effect on how well students learn.

Teachers' Responsibilities Continue to Grow

In the past, teachers were considered good at their jobs if they kept order in the classroom and graded their students fairly. That's no longer the case. While teaching is just one facet of an educational environment that determines the quality of education a child receives, it is an important one. Today's teachers bring much more than just a multicultural knowledge of the subjects to their classrooms. They also bring an awareness of the tremendous differences children exhibit in the way they learn.

For example, some children are naturally competitive and like to work independently, while some need more structure and prefer to work in groups. Some students have shorter attention spans, while others resent having to stop working on something they're engrossed in to skip to something else.

Watch and Learn

Not everyone learns at the same pace. Likewise, different groups of people have their own style of learning. For example, many American Indian cultures value the importance of visualization in learning. Children usually acquire the various skills of their culture in a three-part process. First, the child just watches as an adult performs the entire task. Then the child begins to take over small portions of the task under the supervision of the adult, gradually learning all the different components of the project. Only then does the child go off by himself to perform the task and then bring it back to show the teacher and other adults to see if the skill has been properly learned. There is very little talk in this process; the child is supposed to learn by watching. In contrast, most *mainstream* American schools place a high value on verbal performance: asking questions, learning from the verbal presentations of teachers, volunteering answers in class.

Some students learn better when audio-visual materials are used in class. Some lack self-confidence and need lots of feedback and support from their teachers. Others like to ask questions in class, volunteer their own opinions, and discuss and argue the concepts being presented. All of these learning styles are equally valid. If teachers recognize their students' individual learning needs, then can design a teaching style that best reaches everyone.

These aren't the only changes schools are making in how they approach teaching. In the past, schools may have themselves contributed to the sexual stereotyping that was common in the U.S. by subtly treating the boys in their classes differently from the girls. For example, it might not have been unusual to read the back of good female student's report card and see adjectives such as *appreciative*, *calm*, *conscientious*, *considerate*, *cooperative*, *mannerly*, *sensitive*, *dependable*, *efficient*, *mature*, *obliging*, and *thorough*. Adjectives used to describe boys, on the other hand, may have included *active*, *adventurous*, *aggressive*, *assertive*, *curious*, *energetic*, *enterprising*, *frank*, *independent*, and *inventive*. In a subtle way, girls may have received approval for passive and conforming behavior, while boys were rewarded for being independent and aggressive.

The way girls and women were depicted in books written for school children also strongly reinforced this type of stereotyping. Although textbooks have certainly changed over the last few decades, recent studies show that books about boys still outnumber books about girls almost three to one. Much of the fiction written about girls still trivializes and demeans women by suggesting that their most important concerns are their relationships with the opposite sex. Aware teachers are helping to change these stereotypes by using textbooks and other classroom materials that appropriately reflect equal expectations for both girls and boys.

Teaching a Multicultural Curriculum

All subjects, but history in particular, can be viewed from more than a single perspective. For example, on December 7, 1941, Japanese armed forces

To really understand how an event like Pearl Harbor affected U.S. history, students study all viewpoints, including those of the thousands of Japanese-Americans who, like these citizens lined up for a meal, were forcibly interned in government detention camps during WWII.

attacked the U.S. naval base at Pearl Harbor. By the evening of the same day, the FBI had picked up six hundred Japanese immigrants and forced them into detention centers. Two months later, President Franklin D. Roosevelt signed Executive Order 9066, which authorized government officials to relocate *all* people of Japanese ancestry living on the West Coast (even if they were American citizens) into internment camps from 1942 to 1945.

In the 1950s and 1960s, most students were taught the traditional, monocultural view of this mass relocation of people. They were taught that the U.S. government had no choice — we were at war with Japan and these people had to be interned for reasons of national security. Textbooks showed pictures and described the horrors of the Pearl Harbor bombings and other Japanese wartime atrocities. While these helped make the actions of an outraged and fearful government understandable, this is far from being the only view of what happened during this time in U.S. history. The reality was that 120,000 people of Japanese ancestry were forced from their homes into prison camps. Their personal possessions were either permanently confiscated by government officials or sold at auction. What is especially important to note is that over 60 percent of these people were American citizens.

Today, more teachers and textbooks examine this historical event in a way that is multicultural in its point of view and closer to the truth. Students study pictures and read firsthand accounts about what the relocated Japanese-American families had to go through: the living conditions in the *nisei* detention camps, the loss of their property and civil rights, the humiliation and discrimination they felt long after the war was over. They learn why Japanese immigrants chose to come to the U.S. in the first place and what their experiences were not just during the war, but beforehand, and what it's like to be a Japanese-American now. Many teachers expand this lesson even further to include the different feelings within the Japanese community between older Japanese-Americans and a younger generation born after the war, now that the U.S. government has finally started making reparations to the thousands who were interned more than fifty years ago. By studying history from a multicultural perspective, each student in the class can better identify and understand that history is neither a glorification of right and wrong nor a lesson in blind patriotism, but a study of why events happened and how they affected everyone.

Many teachers enrich all of their classes with a multicultural approach. For example, if their students study U.S. involvement in the Mexican-American War, they'll also take time to learn about Mexican-American culture, its traditional food and clothing styles, religious beliefs, important contributions to music and literature, art, and the theater, the traditional roles of men and women in these cultures and how they have evolved over the years, important political movements — in short, what it meant to be a part of this culture then, and what it means now.

Teachers know a lot more about social studies and history than they ever did before. This is a tremendous challenge. Not only are teachers today more aware of how the students in their classroom relate culturally and individually to each other, they also have a special understanding of the physical, emotional, or mental challenges each student brings to the learning process, and how best to offer special students the individual attention they need. Instead of standing in front of their class and reciting lessons, teachers today may use a wide variety of methods and materials that many students simply take for granted.

Almost as much fun as a video arcade, computer technology opens up whole new worlds of learning in every subject from Japanese grammar to musical notation to aerodynamic design.

This may mean rearranging classroom desks to accommodate both group and individual learning projects, scheduling field trips, and creating special community-related projects — in other words, doing whatever they feel is necessary to make learning interesting and relevant to every member of the class.

Learning activities may include having the class read magazines and newspapers, view videos or listen to audiotapes or CDs, conduct experiments, do ecology projects, interview members of the community, play games, practice role playing and communication skills, use a computer, and learn about new cultures by celebrating a variety of ethnic holidays and festivities.

Teachers encourage students to try out a number of ways of self-expression, including writing, acting, creating music, and drawing. They teach them how to work in groups and how to work on independent assignments outside of class. Modern teachers go beyond teaching a national perspective to emphasize

Computers go to the head of the class

Using computers in the classroom has not only made math and science more fun and learning a foreign language much easier, it is an exciting way to provide equal learning opportunities to people with physical disabilities. The Consortium for School Networking (known as EDUCOM) is a Washington-based group of educational institutions and corporations that have come together to promote the use of computer technology in education. They estimate that about 4.3 million students in U.S. elementary and high schools have special physical needs that can be successfully addressed with computers and related devices. Such devices include pressure-sensitive switches, headwands, touch-sensitive tablets, voice-recognition systems, mouthsticks, Braille screens and printers, large-screen displays, and even devices that read the contents of a computer screen out loud. Computers can bring speech and phone use to people who are nonverbal or hearing impaired. In some places, computer technology is already being made available to preschoolers. Many children with serious disabilities become frustrated because they have no way of expressing themselves. Computers give them a way. Equally exciting is that computers allow students to work with greater independence and self-esteem. And as with computers that are used in regular class work, as wonderful and liberating as the technology may be, it is still the *students* who do the thinking, creating, and problem solving.

the history of cultures throughout the world. By introducing their students to global problems of poverty and world hunger, environmental crises, overpopulation, war, and nuclear weapons, they help American children understand how all people are united in a global community whose problems affect every person on earth.

Developing Multicultural Textbooks. It is estimated that 80-90 percent of U.S. school curriculums rely on textbooks — more than schools in any other country. By the time most students complete high school, they will have read over thirty-two thousand textbook pages, so it is understandable that parents and educators are concerned about the political, social, and cultural values that textbooks portray.

The U.S. Commission on Civil Rights found a disturbing number of inaccuracies and omissions regarding how cultural groups were being portrayed in textbooks before 1980. For example, African-Americans were often portrayed as servants or in other stereotyped service roles, or as sports or entertainment figures. There was little description given in U.S. history books to the actual conditions in which Blacks have had to live and work throughout the nation's history.

Textbooks were equally lacking when it came to their treatment of American Indian cultures. They rarely portrayed the rich diversity of tribal cultures and traditions, and there is almost no discussion at all of American Indian life in the twentieth century. Textbooks written before 1980 also failed to include an account of this country's events and experiences (such as the arrival of European traders or the country's westward expansion) from an American Indian perspective.

The commission's study found that Cuban-, Mexican-, and Puerto Rican-Americans were often lumped together under one cultural heading in textbooks, and that they were generally depicted as living in poverty in segregated neighborhoods. Hispanic groups were also often depicted as prone to violent behavior.

Asian-Americans and Pacific Islanders, when mentioned at all in textbooks, were most commonly portrayed doing service work, such as operating laundries and restaurants, or working on railroad crews.

Older people were commonly described as small, dependent, sickly, and often senile, and the impression was usually given that old age is not an enjoyable time of life — or that older people have little that is constructive to offer society.

The list of inaccuracies the commission found goes on to include many other ethnic and cultural groups, as well as women, people with disabilities, and members of numerous religious groups. While the inaccuracies, biased language, and significant omissions in textbooks have certainly decreased since 1980, teachers are aware that curriculum changes are an ongoing process and use a variety of sources and methods to present their multicultural material to students.

Special and Gifted Education in a Multicultural Society. Today's teachers also face other challenges. It is estimated that almost one out of every ten school-age children in this country (about five million elementary and secondary students) needs some type of special education services. About 86 percent of this group are learning disabled, speech impaired, or mentally retarded children, 8 percent are emotionally disturbed, and the remainder have visual, hearing, orthopedic, or other conditions. As a result of the legislation passed on the behalf of people with disabilities since the 1960s, the federal government has legally guaranteed the right of disabled children to receive an equal opportunity in U.S. schools. The Education for All Handicapped Students Act of 1975, for example, sets guidelines for assessment tests that ensure that the child is tested in his or her native language and is given more than one type of test to determine placement for special education needs.

The act also guarantees that parents have access to all school records of the child and that they have the right to question the school's assessment processes. It further guarantees that the child is placed in the least restrictive educational setting (that is, offered the chance to participate as much as possible with regular-education students), and that all students with special needs receive an individualized, written description of their education plan that includes how they are to be evaluated.

The Education for All Handicapped Students Act of 1975 ensures the right of children with physical and intellectual disabilities to participate in "mainstream" classroom settings with other students.

Controversial Issues in Modern Education

While almost everyone agrees that U.S. schools should offer every student equal educational opportunities, there is still a great deal of controversy as to how that can best be achieved. School policy is now a major concern of both local and national politicians, and many issues that are not decided in the polls are decided in the nation's courts. These issues are not limited to evaluating textbooks and teaching methods. Problems concern a wide range of social difficulties that affect education, including poverty, crime, taxation, employment, equal rights, academic freedom, racial integration, religious freedom, and school disciplinary action. There is also controversy over whether these are national issues, or whether they are best worked out on a state or even community basis.

Paying for the Education of Noncitizens. One issue that continues to generate controversy, especially along the Mexican-American border, is the education of undocumented foreign-born children in U.S. public schools. This problem does not just concern the children of people who entered the U.S. illegally and now make this country their home. Many noncitizens choose to give birth to their children in U.S. hospitals even though they do not intend to make the U.S. their home. Children who are born on U.S. soil are automatically considered U.S. citizens — citizens who are entitled to free, public tuition. When Texas tried to exclude such children from its public school system in 1982, the Supreme Court prevented it from doing so by ruling that all children are entitled to tuition-free education, whether or not they are citizens. That decision is still being fought in a number of states, including California.

Expanding the Curriculum to Help Disadvantaged Students. Studies conducted in the 1960s and 1970s showed that students from low-income families, children of the urban poor, and the children of African-American, American Indian, or Mexican families were more likely to have problems keeping up in school and were therefore more likely to drop out. These controversial studies recommended that it was the responsibility of the school systems and the federal government to establish special educational projects to help such disadvantaged students have a more equal chance at succeeding in school. Project Head Start, Vista, the Job Corps, Teachers Corp, and Upward Bound were some of the federally funded projects that social-minded politicians helped pass through Congress.

While liberal supporters claimed that these programs helped low-income and minority students without taking anything away from other students,

Children born on U.S. soil are considered U.S. citizens, even if their parents are non-citizens. In areas north of the Mexican border, this entitles U.S.-born children of Mexican parents to the same education that any other American-born child would receive.

Many inner-city teachers like Marva Collins of Chicago refuse to give up on so-called problem children. Her students, kicked out of other public schools, are now reading Shakespeare and Aristotle.

The AIDS battle reaches into middle schools

In late 1993, health clinics in New Haven, Connecticut, middle schools began providing condoms to students who requested them. The school board voted to take this highly controversial measure because of the grim realities of city life. At least 833 cases of full-blown AIDS had been diagnosed in New Haven, with 203 of them diagnosed in the six months prior to instituting the new program. Because of the disease's long incubation period, it is believed that many more people in New Haven, and elsewhere throughout the U.S., are unknowingly carrying the virus. Critics of the measure are concerned that the school system's action sends the message to children of eighth-grade age and younger that having sex is okay. Supporters of the measure point out that a 1992 survey indicated that a disturbing 27 percent of sixth graders and 49 percent of eighth graders in New Haven schools reported that they had already had sexual intercourse. They believe that however uncomfortable the public was with these statistics, they had a moral obligation to act on them.

critics of the programs claimed that it was not the job of the schools (or of the U.S. government) to change society through social-action programs and that the programs made little difference anyway. Politicians are still debating the funding cutbacks that put an end to most of these programs during the Reagan administration.

Many social activists also promote another controversial issue in public schools: sex education. They feel that sex education is a necessary part of a school curriculum in an age of widespread AIDS and venereal disease. They point to the soaring number of babies born to unmarried high school students and the increasing national divorce rate. They also recommend that sex education be expanded in more schools from the discussion of reproduction in biology classes to separate class discussions of dating, marriage, parenthood, child care, health, and social responsibility.

The "New Right" and a Return to Conservative Values. On the conservative end of the political spectrum is the political and religious movement that emerged in the 1980s and, calling itself the New Right, fought for these funding cutbacks. Members of this movement believe that U.S. schools should return to more conservative educational programs that promote moral character, patriotism, strict discipline, and respect for authority. Many of them oppose a multicultural approach to the curriculum because they believe it promotes the splitting of U.S. society into separate (and hostile) ethnic groups, rather than molding everyone into a homogenized American ideal. They prefer that children be taught a set of values that clearly shows them what is right and wrong, rather than be encouraged to develop their own moral consciences. Under this philosophy, many oppose sex education in the schools, advocate the teaching of the Biblical story of creation to balance the theory of evolution, and urge a return to allowing prayer in the schools.

Teacher Competency Tests. Throughout the history of U.S. schools, when students in a particular school system tested lower than the national average, many concerned parents reacted by blaming the teachers. The idea that teachers are directly accountable for the education each of their students receive (including those who are culturally different, non-English-speaking, or physically, mentally, or emotionally exceptional) continues to be a hotly debated issue in the 1990s.

Many other people believe it is not always fair to blame a student's poor school performance on the teacher — that parents, other students, community organizations, media, and even the federal government should also be held accountable. They point out that in many communities teachers are given little voice in determining the direction of their work and have little if any input as to what they're supposed to teach or even which textbooks they are allowed to use. Some school systems have gone so far as to propose that teachers be paid only in accordance with how well their students perform on certain assessment tests every year, a practice many teachers compare to paying doctors only if their patients survive.

Private Schools and the Voucher System. Cutbacks in federal and state funding in the last few decades have hit schools hard, especially in poorer urban areas. Many more affluent parents who are concerned about the quality of public education are pulling their children out of the public school system and enrolling them instead in expensive, privately run schools. As a result, other, less affluent parents feel it is unfair that they don't have the same

Should we flunk our teachers?

In the 1970s, many critics of the quality of U.S. schools focused on the role of teachers, blaming teaching competency for the poor performance of their students. California went so far as to pass the California Stull Act, which requires that teacher competency be measured in part by the performance scores of their pupils. Many teachers' groups feel this is unfair, and as a result, teacher accountability is still an important issue in almost every state. It has even been tested in the courts. In 1976, a student sued the San Francisco Unified School District for allowing him to graduate high school although he could only read at a sixth-grade proficiency level. His lawyers claimed that it was the fault of his teachers for not realizing and correcting his learning problem long before he graduated.

choices for their children. Although the more affluent parents can afford private schools, many feel it is only fair that the money the government would have spent educating their children in public school be applied to private-school costs instead. And many of the less affluent parents who want their kids in private schools also believe the government should fund at least part of their child's private school education.

One idea these parents have proposed to make this work is called the voucher system. Theoretically, if a state passed laws approving such a system, every student in private or parochial school would be eligible for a voucher (some people call it a "scholarship") each year equal to either the per-pupil amount the state was spending on education that year, or a lesser agreed-upon amount. While that may sound fair on the surface, critics of voucher systems point out that such a system would immediately cause some serious problems. California, which came close to passing such as system in late 1992 with its Proposition 174, is a good example.

It is estimated that in the mid-1990s, one out of every four California public school children came from a family on welfare, that nearly half of those who entered the first grade came from a home where little or no English is spoken, and that more than 55 percent of the students were Hispanic-, African-, or Asian-American. As the percentage of poor and minority children in California schools increased over the past few decades, the per-pupil amount the state was spending on education decreased sharply and is now estimated at about $5,200. If passed, Proposition 174 would have provided half that amount ($2,600) to every student enrolled in a private or parochial school. This would have cut down substantially on the amount of money available to the state for its public schools.

Critics of this voucher system pointed out that there were no restrictions at all on the kind of schools that would be eligible. Parents would receive the voucher amount whether the school they chose was run by the local Catholic archdiocese, the Flat Earth Society, or the witches of the Contra Costa Pagan Association (who had, in fact, announced that they would immediately start their own school if the voucher system were passed).

Another problem critics pointed to was the issue of discrimination. Proposition 174 did stipulate that the private school could not discriminate on the basis of race or ethnic background. However, discrimination on the basis of gender, disability, sexual orientation, and religion *was* permitted, and any student "deriving no substantial academic benefit" could be dismissed (in effect, thrown out) by the private school at any time. That meant that any school that didn't want to deal with the children who are usually the most expensive to educate — kids with learning disabilities, those who speak little or no English, those who are unmotivated or emotionally troubled — did not have to accept them. (After all, critics argue, why would these schools voluntarily take a child whose schooling costs more than $15,000 a year, as the education of many special education students does, and give him or her a place in their school for only $2,600?) For many kids, critics argued, this meant that under a voucher system, it was the schools and not the parents who

The best education is one that allows each child to grow to his or her full potential.

really had the choice. This system would also make the public schools responsible for educating the most expensive to educate, the very system that was already strapped for funds.

Home Schooling. Another alternative to what many see as the declining quality of traditional public education is home schooling. This does not just mean a system in which parents keep their children at home and educate them themselves. Instead, it is an open, loosely structured classroom setting in which the children of a number of families meet on a daily basis to learn. Home schooling stresses student individuality and social interaction. Some schools, like the Open Alternative School in Sebostapol, California, employ a former public school teacher to teach a group of children ranging in age from kindergarten level to third grade.

In others, one of the parents gives up a paying job to stay at home and teach. Instead of using traditional textbooks, students meet with their instructors to decide their own classroom schedule and what materials they will study. In addition to learning reading skills, they spend class time discussing their own individual issues, working out any playground or other social problems they might have, and comment about community and world

Some home schools get a helping hand

In some areas, the public school systems are voting to work with home schools instead of in competition with them. In Santa Rosa, California, for example, a home school program that was organized to teach students in kindergarten through the sixth grade became so popular that its enrollment grew to 240 pupils. In 1991, the school board in Santa Rosa voted to share some of its operating funds (up to one thousand dollars per pupil) with the home schooling system to help cover expenses for textbooks and other teaching materials, and to give the parents who were acting as teachers at least a small salary to compensate their efforts. They also offered the home school system access to various public school activities, such as vision and hearing screening, the library, and school photo day.

issues and how to solve them. They are also encouraged to experiment with a number of ways of expressing themselves, including art, music, and writing. The teacher's job in home schooling classrooms is to teach the students, not to discipline or control them, which usually gives students a lot more freedom than they would find in traditional, public classrooms. Critics of home schooling are afraid that these students are getting less than a high-quality academic education.

Today, many students from Latin- or Asian-American backgrounds require education in more than one language. Even in colonial times, immigrant communities attended schools taught in their native languages – often in German, Polish, or Swedish.

Bilingual Education. Before the 1960s, most states required that public school instruction be given only in English. Civil rights groups, however, began calling attention to the large numbers of students who were failing or dropping out of school because they could not speak or understand English. This was especially true in Texas, where many Spanish-speaking students entered schools in which teachers spoke no Spanish. Because of the attention civil rights groups drew to this problem, the Bilingual Education Act was passed in 1968, approving over $160 million for bilingual programs over the next eleven years. Under the act, children whose native language was not English were to receive instruction in two languages. The law, which was upheld in a Supreme Court decision in 1974, still stands, although the federal funding for these programs was reduced in the budget cuts of the Reagan administration.

Many people in the United States who are opposed to the concept of bilingual education argue that other immigrants came to this country without knowing any English, were only taught English in the public schools they attended, and (supposedly) never had any problems. This sink-or-swim approach implies that the faster students are exposed to English, the faster and better they'll learn it. Although many immigrant children may have succeeded under these circumstances, many more did not. Immigration statistics show that almost half of the children from non-English-speaking families who immigrated to the U.S. between 1900 and 1910, for example, were at least one grade behind in school. Two-thirds of these immigrant children dropped out of school before their junior year of high school.

Another misconception some people have is that all language-minority students (people whose first language is not English) are fairly recent immigrants. In reality, many cultural groups in the U.S. (some Asian-American and Hispanic-American groups, for example) have continued to use their language on a community and family level. Many of the children in these communities learn little or no English until they begin public school.

Some critics of bilingual education like to point out that minority groups today don't have the right to demand bilingual educational programs because throughout the history of the U.S. no other minority groups ever made such demands. They are unaware of the fact that the U.S. has a long tradition of using languages other then English for instructional purposes, especially in colonial times, when religious schools in German, Polish, and Scandinavian communities were taught in the native immigrant language. These immigrant groups certainly wanted their children to learn the language of their new, adopted country (English), but at the same time, they did not want them to lose the language and culture of their ancestry, either. The only difference now is that the emphasis is on Hispanic, Asian, and American Indian languages.

Multiculturalism in the Curriculum. One of the most rewarding — and often controversial — components of multicultural education is the need to present historical events from all perspectives, rather than from a single "true" perspective. Some critics argue that while teaching from a multicultural perspective gives lots of attention to the history and cultures of minorities, it ignores the accomplishments of Western civilization that came to America from Europe. These critics also feel that multiculturalism wrongly promotes a view of America as a collection of many unrelated cultures rather than a single, *united* culture with a single, united history.

This criticism of multiculturalism in the schools is understandable. Throughout the history of education in the U.S., many have felt that the dominant (that is, European-American) culture is the most important culture and that it should therefore receive most of the attention. Many still feel this way today, especially those who think that European-American culture is being ignored by the multicultural curriculum. Unfortunately, however, teaching American history from the traditional viewpoint of the European-American majority has left many gaps in our understanding of how America and the world have come to be as they are today.

Multiculturalism helps us fill in those gaps. For example, it teaches us about the genocidal acts committed against American Indians by European settlers and the U.S. government from the time of Columbus through the twentieth century. It teaches us about the horrors of slavery and of subjecting African-Americans to continued "legal" discrimination for a hundred years following the war to end slavery. It teaches us about wars waged against people and nations in Latin America by North Americans bent on getting as much land and power as they could grab. It teaches us about the unjust detention of Americans during World War II for the "crime" of being of Japanese descent and looking "different." However unsavory, these are significant events in our history.

Multiculturalism also opens our eyes to the efforts made by people from all cultures to bridge these gaps, fight slavery, rise against intolerance, and right the wrongs committed throughout our history. Multicultural education helps us recognize — and accept — the challenge to reveal history not just as reported by the dominant culture but as it continues to be lived by us all.

1635	Boston Latin Grammar School is founded
1647	Massachusetts law of 1647 makes establishment of schools mandatory
1649	Society for the Propagation of the Gospel establishes Indian praying towns
1682	Jesuits who accompany French set up missions to educate Indian children
1751	Benjamin Franklin establishes the first academy in the U.S.
1760	Spanish Franciscan missionaries establish missions in the Southwest to convert Indians
1805	Public School Society of New York founded
1808	First Jewish school in U.S. established
1817	Gallaudet begins the first education of the deaf in the U.S. in Hartford, Connecticut
1818	First Infant School is founded in Boston
1819	Congress establishes Civilization Fund; leads to boarding schools for Indian children
1821	First high school founded in the U.S.
1827	Massachusetts law passed making establishment of high schools mandatory
1829	Georgia passes law making it illegal to educate African-Americans (free or slave)
1839	First normal school in U.S. established in Lexington, Massachusetts
1849	Supreme Court upholds segregation of schools in *Boston v. Roberts*
1850s-1920s	Orphan Trains resettle orphaned immigrant children with families in the West
1851	First education begun in U.S. for people with mental disabilities (Massachusetts)
1852	Massachusetts passes law making education compulsory
1855	First U.S. kindergarten (taught in German) started in Wisconsin; Freedmen's Bureau created to promote African-American education
1861	Outbreak of the U.S. Civil War; Freedman's Bureau created to promote education for African-Americans
1872	Government turns over responsibility for Indian education to religious organizations
1909	First classes for people with speech disabilities organized in New York; W. E. B. Du Bois helps found Niagra Movement and the National Association for the Advancement for Colored People (NAACP); first White House Conferences on Children held
1917	The Smith-Hughes Act is passed, encouraging vocational education in the United States
1919-1950	Progressive Education Movement in U.S.
1944-1946	Congress passes G.I. Bill providing for the education of World War II veterans
1954	U.S. Supreme Court requires racial integration in public schools
1957	Federal troops are sent into Little Rock, Arkansas, to enforce court-ordered integration
1962	James Meredith becomes first African-American student admitted to University of Mississippi
1964	Congress passes Civil Rights Act and Economic Opportunity Act
1965	Elementary and Secondary Education Act provides financial aid to local school districts; Congress passes Higher Education Act of 1965

1968	Bilingual Education Act is passed
1970s	Founding of the Native American Rights Fund, the Puerto Rican Legal Defense and Education Fund, and the Mexican-American Legal Defense and Education Fund
1972	Education Amendments Act
1975	Education for All Handicapped Children Act is passed
1980s	Spending cuts under Reagan Administration slash many educational programs started in the 1950s, 1960s, and 1970s
1990	Americans with Disabilities Act is passed

GLOSSARY

abolitionist societies	pre-Civil War antislavery organizations that worked to educate African-Americans
adventure schools	girls schools established in urban areas of northern colonies
African free schools	nineteenth-century schools run by free Blacks for free Blacks
apprentice system	colonial system in which boys worked with craftsmen to learn a trade
baby boom	increase in birthrate following World War II that led to need for more schools
camp schools	nineteenth-century schools that followed railroad, mining, and logging crews
charity schools	schools for orphans and paupers in the southern colonies
clandestine schools	secret nineteenth-century schools for African-Americans held in the homes of abolitionists
dame schools	colonial schools held in homes of school teachers for boys and girls
de facto segregation	separate public facilities for different racial groups in spite of laws prohibiting segregation by race; usually occurs in neighborhoods that are already racially segregated
de jure segregation	separate public facilities for different racial groups ordered by law
Five Civilized Tribes	the Cherokee, Choctaw, Creek, Chickasaw, and Seminole; so-called because of their decision to adopt many facets of European-American culture; located in Southeast before being relocated to Indian Territory in the 1830s
Franciscans	eighteenth-century Spanish Catholic missionaries in Southwest
Freedmen's Bureau	federal organization created during Civil War to educate African-Americans
Freedom Riders	civil rights activists who traveled through the South in the 1960s
G.I. Bill	post WWII bill enacted by Congress to subsidize veteran education
Indian Removal Act	1830 federal legislation ordering the removal of Indian tribes in the eastern U.S. to specially created Indian Territory in Oklahoma

Indian boarding schools   mandatory nineteenth-century government schools for Indian children

infant schools   first schools in U.S. for very young children, established in 1818

Jesuits   eighteenth-century French Catholic missionaries who attempted to convert Great Lakes and Plains Indians

Ku Klux Klan   secret racist societies started in 1866 and revived in 1915

Latin grammar schools   secondary schools set up in Middle Atlantic colonies to prepare more affluent male students for college

Niagra Movement   organization founded by W. E. B. Du Bois in 1905 to promote African-American equality

old field schools   schools run in southern colonies to teach local poor European-American children

orphan trains   nineteenth-century program to resettle orphaned immigrant children in the West

Pan-Indian Movement   early twentieth-century movement to promote equality of American Indians

praying towns   colonial settlements to protect converted Algonquin and Iroquois

Progressive Movement   association of private, experimental schools in U.S. from 1919 to 1950

termination   1950s relocation of Indians from reservations to cities

voucher system   a system in which the government contributes a certain amount of money to parents who pay to send their children to private schools

FURTHER READING

Brown, Dee. *Wondrous Times on the Frontier*. New York: Harper Collins, 1992.

Erdoes, Richard and Ortiz, Alfonso, eds. *American Indian Myths and Legends*. New York: Pantheon Books, 1984.

Fischel, Jack and Pinsker, Sanford, editors. *Jewish-American History and Culture : An Encyclopedia*. New York: Garland, 1992.

Fischer, Renate and Lane, Harlan, eds. *Looking Back: A Reader on the History of Deaf Communities and Their Sign Languages*. Hamburg: Signum Press, 1993.

Nabokov, Peter. *Native American Testimony (A Chronicle of Indian-White Relations from Prophecy to the Present, 1492-1992)*. New York: Viking Penguin, 1991.

Namiamas, June. First Generation: *In the Words of Twentieth-Century American Immigrants*. Urbana: University of Illinois Press, 1992.

Riley, Patricia, editor. *Growing Up Native American: An Anthology*. New York: William Morrow, 1993.

Takaki, Ronald. *A Different Mirror: A History of Multicultural America*. Boston: Little, Brown and Company, 1993.

Tateishi, John. *And Justice For All : An Oral History of the Japanese American Detention Camps*. New York: Random House, 1984.

Wexler, Sanford. *The Civil Rights Movement: An Eyewitness History*. New York: Facts on File, 1993.